METAPHYSICS

METAPHYSICS

An Introduction to Contemporary
Debates and Their History

ANNA MARMODORO AND
ERASMUS MAYR

OXFORD
UNIVERSITY PRESS

OXFORD

UNIVERSITY PRESS

Oxford University Press is a department of the University of Oxford. It furthers
the University's objective of excellence in research, scholarship, and education
by publishing worldwide. Oxford is a registered trade mark of Oxford University
Press in the UK and certain other countries.

Published in the United States of America by Oxford University Press
198 Madison Avenue, New York, NY 10016, United States of America.

© Oxford University Press 2019

CIP data is on file at the Library of Congress
ISBN 978-0-19-094162-8 (pbk.)
ISBN 978-0-19-094161-1 (hbk.)

To our young friends
Lisa, Lisa, and Anna.

CONTENTS

ACKNOWLEDGMENTS

This book project began as a philosophical conversation between two colleagues and friends, whose agreements and disagreements with respect to metaphysical matters sparked off many lively discussions to "work things out"— to understand each other's point of view better, to seek common ground, to reach conclusions, or take stock if ultimate conclusions could not be reached. It is in the spirit of a conversation that involves the reader too, that this book was written. Our goal is ultimately to introduce the reader to core philosophical questions, and to examine *with her or him* the arguments with which the questions have been addressed, in current as well as past debates that have shaped the history of metaphysics.

We are grateful to all our colleagues and students who at different stage of the project have enriched our conversation with their contributions, questions, and objections—George Darby, Andrea Roselli and Konstantin Weber in particular.

We want to extend our warmest thanks also to OUP's book readers: John Heil and a second reader who remained anonymous; and to the Editor, Peter Ohlin. This book has grown from our earlier work, Marmodoro and Mayr (2017), on which Gianluca Mori from Carocci Editore kindly allowed us to draw. Last but not least, we are grateful to Gianluca Mori and our wonderful Italian publisher Carroci, who allowed / encouraged us to use, as a basis of this book, the text of our Italian book 'Breve introduzione alla metafisica' (Rome: Carocci 2017). It is from modifications and additions to this text that the present book has developed – we hope the two years' more thinking have not been in vain.

INTRODUCTION

What is metaphysics about?

THE DESIRE TO UNDERSTAND HOW things are, why they are as they are, and why they change is deeply rooted in human nature. This desire has expressed itself in two main forms of systematic inquiry in the history of human thought: on the one hand, in the empirical way of science, and, on the other hand, in the speculative way of philosophy. While philosophy has been concerned with many different questions—such as how we should live or whether we can know anything—one particular line of philosophical inquiry, since antiquity, has been about investigating the fundamental make-up of reality. This branch of philosophical inquiry is called metaphysics. The word itself (even if Aristotle did not use it) derives from the title of one of Aristotle's works. It was an editor (in all probability, Andronicus of Rhodes), at least one hundred years after Aristotle's death, who titled one of his works "*Ta meta ta physika*," meaning literally "the [books] after the physical ones," where the "physical ones" are the collection of books that we now call Aristotle's *Physics*. While the domain of interest of metaphysics has steadily evolved since Aristotle's time, there is also a continuity between ancient and contemporary metaphysics in subject matter and methodology.

Like other sciences, contemporary metaphysics has goals and characteristic methods: in very broad terms, its aim is to advance our understanding of reality by analyzing problems and developing explanations, which are then "tested", for example, against possible counterexamples that the proposed account might not be able to explain. In other respects, however, metaphysics is essentially different from other sciences. Metaphysics aims at what is most general and fundamental, in terms of its questions as well as its answers: its domain is *what there is*, or we could say, *all there is*. As Aristotle put it, metaphysics tries to discover the first principles and causes of everything, and is concerned with "being as such". These two features, fundamentality and generality, distinguish the science of metaphysics from other sciences. Take biology, for instance, the science concerned with *living* beings. The principles which biology wants to discover are neither fundamental nor general ones. Consider: a biologist sets out to discover and finds a biological law L_B that explains how the offspring of a certain species inherits certain traits from their parents. The biologist's expectation will be that either L_B is explicable in terms of an even more fundamental law of chemistry L_C (which allows us to understand exactly how the traits' transmission mechanism works), or, at the very least, the transmission procedure must accord with more fundamental laws of chemistry L_C and ultimately the fundamental laws of physics. In either case, L_B is not truly a "first principle," but less fundamental relative to the relevant laws of chemistry and physics. Furthermore, not all things fall within the purview of biology (e.g., inorganic matter does not), so biology is certainly not concerned with "being as such", that is, the being of all beings.

It is important to note that what is distinctive of metaphysics isn't just that metaphysics spans *everything*. There is, or could be, some other science whose domain is everything that *de facto* exists and whose principles and laws cannot be explained in terms of anything more fundamental than them. Some think that physics is such a science, assuming that nothing but physical objects exists, and that the ultimate physical laws cannot be explained in terms of any more fundamental ones. But even if physics turned out to have everything that exists as its subject matter (and there are very good reasons to doubt that), metaphysics would still remain as a distinct (and we submit, necessary) kind of inquiry into the nature of reality whose investigation cannot be exhaustively carried out by physics alone. First, physics is not concerned with everything *qua existent*, and therefore is not concerned with "being as such," but rather, with things *qua* physical objects. Since even someone who denied that any nonphysical things existed would have to admit that other nonphysical things *might* exist, or there might be some features of reality which are not physical, she would have to admit that studying physical reality is not the same as studying "being as such". Furthermore, that everything which exists is physical, (if it turned out be the the case) is something that could at best be discovered as a result of philosophical and scientific inquiry, and definitely could not be the starting point of an inquiry into what exists. For there is no obvious and immediately compelling reason to assume that only physical things can exist. In order to be able to answer (in the positive) the question of whether all things that exist are physical, we would have to turn to more basic questions first, such as what it means to exist, or what kind of things could in principle exist (only particular things, or also general properties? and can the second exist without the first?, etc.). For without an answer to these questions, physics or any other empirical science could tell us nothing about what we should believe exists.[1] Answering these more "basic" questions, and thereby providing the framework *within* which questions about the scope of physics, and in particular, the question of whether everything that exists is physical, can sensibly be addressed, is the task of—metaphysics.[2] What is distinctive about metaphysical inquiry is therefore not just the *de facto* generality of its subject matter: it is that this generality follows from its attempt to answer fundamental questions about reality, on the basis of which more specific ones can be dealt with in the other sciences.

But one might ask: does such a general and fundamental line of inquiry even make sense? Why should we assume that there is a general and fundamental structure of reality that we can discover or at least search for? The answer is that we cannot really avoid making the assumption that there is some such structure of reality. For ultimately, whenever we think about reality, we must assume that there is just one reality, just as there is only one truth. As Jonathan Lowe put it: "Truth is single and indivisible, or, to put it another way,

---

1. As Lowe (2002, 10) succinctly puts it: "Empirical evidence cannot be evidence for the existence of anything which is not a *possible* feature of reality."

2. Some philosophers have argued that the scope of metaphysics is so encompassing that even the status of metaphysics itself is a metaphysical question, and, as a consequence, it doesn't even make sense to deny the possibility of metaphysics (see Moore 2012, 3; Lowe 2002, 3).

the world or reality as a whole is unitary and necessarily self-consistent."[3] We may not find out very much about how reality is—but at the very least, we must assume that everything we can really find out "fits together". This holds as well for what any science—be it physics, biology, or any other—can tell us: if their findings and theories are correct, then they are all describing aspects of one and the same reality, and therefore cannot contradict one another.

So, at the very least, this much, namely the existence and consistency of one basic and general structure of reality, is something any inquiry about the world must be based on. But as we are going to see in the following chapters, there is good reason to be even more optimistic and to think that by means of philosophical inquiry we can discover more than such an extremely "thin" structure of reality. For very often, when reflecting on certain things whose truth we are very confident about, we find out that in order to make sense of these things, we have to assume (or it is best to assume) that there is some underlying structure or some underlying categories which explain this truth. For instance, you will be very confident that there is a book in front of you, and it will be extremely hard to convince you otherwise. When you make a coffee stain on one of its pages, you will be equally confident that it is still the same book, even though something about it has changed. Thinking about these matters—that something remains the same in some way even through a perceived change—makes it very natural to distinguish two fundamental categories, namely of substance, and of its properties, where the former can remain the same, even though some

3. Lowe (2002, 3).

of the properties it has might change. (We will discuss this issue at more length in chapter 1.) In what follows, we will introduce other instances of this strategy—and alternative ones—to show that they provide us with good reasons for substantial metaphysical claims.

Thus, some general structure will have to be presupposed for any specific scientific inquiry. Further, this general structure will not be the concern of any particular natural science. For as we have seen, even if it turned out that, as a matter of fact, everything that exists was the object of a particular science, say physics, this would not make the metaphysician's job redundant: even if everything real were physical, physics on its own certainly couldn't tell us so. (Nor, for that matter, could physics itself tell us how it relates to apparently conflicting findings of other sciences, say chemistry or biology, because physics is only able to adjudicate questions about things *qua* physical beings.[4]) Metaphysicians should not therefore worry that their subject matter will be "taken over" by the natural sciences, or that what is not covered by the natural sciences will be unworthy of investigation. This was a common enough worry in the heyday of scientism in the twentieth century—and, at the same time, a widespread hope among philosophers hostile to traditional metaphysics, who thought that the important questions about the structure of reality, such as they were, would be left to the sciences.[5] This worry is as empty as the opposite hope (namely

4. For more on the need for metaphysics to "adjudicate" between the different disciplines and sciences see Lowe (2002, 2f).

5. Just as one example of this view see the following statement of W. V. O. Quine: "It is within science itself, and not in some prior philosophy, that reality is to be identified and described" (1981, 21).

that philosophy makes the sciences redundant); we reject the idea that metaphysics is just an outdated intellectual inquiry that has been made redundant by the progress of modern science, and we will try to give you in this introduction an insight into how lively and exciting this kind of inquiry still is.

This does not mean, however, that metaphysics could, or should, completely disregard the findings of modern science. If metaphysics is going to help us "make sense" of things in the world, by trying to discover (parts of) the underlying structure of reality, then it should take into account what our best contemporary science tells us about the world. And, indeed, we will see at different points in this book how considerations from modern science are relevant for how to think about the underlying structure of reality, for example by showing us that certain intuitively plausible assumptions about the world (e.g., the connection between powers and qualitative features, section 2.6) need not be ultimately compelling.

When we try to understand what makes metaphysics distinctive, the relation between metaphysics and the natural sciences is only one of the issues. Another one is the relation between metaphysics and our natural language. Just as many scientifically minded philosophers have thought that the "real" questions of traditional metaphysics could be turned over to the natural sciences, because the latter were the ones suited to describe and explain reality, you might think—going into the opposite direction, as it were—that what metaphysics could ever discover could just be the structure of the language we use to think and talk about reality. This view does not deny that there are questions that are, in a sense, more fundamental than those addressed in the sciences, but it does deny that metaphysics can really discover anything *about reality*; it can discover only something about our way of thinking and speaking about reality (which is historically contingent).

Addressing this worry is no less important for an adherent of the "traditional" project of metaphysics than addressing the worry about the relation between metaphysics and the natural sciences. And it is important to stress that metaphysical questions are not just questions about language—if they were, we would most probably arrive at different metaphysical conclusions depending on the languages we contingently speak. So we will have to be very careful about taking peculiarities of linguistic practice (e.g., of grammar) to reflect some underlying feature of reality. But nonetheless, natural language can be an important guide in many cases, since it usually encapsulates ways of thinking about the structure of reality which come naturally to us and which have proved useful and viable over the time the language evolved. This does not mean that ordinary language is "sacrosanct," or that it cannot turn out to be the case that grammatical distinctions do not correspond to distinctions of fact. But ordinary language is usually a good place to start. As John J. L. Austin nicely put it: "Ordinary language is *not* the last word: in principle it can everywhere be supplemented and improved upon and superseded. Only remember, it is the *first* word."[6]

Based on this understanding of the enterprise of metaphysics, this book will give the reader a brief introduction to the subject, with reference to current debates and their historical background. We will focus on the following topics: substance, properties, modality, causality, and free

6. Austin (1979, 185).

will. For reasons of space, and complexity of the issues, we cannot offer a full overview of our five topics and the relevant debates in the literature. However, we hope to give the reader at least a sense of why these issues have fascinated so many generations of philosophers and continue to do so. In addition, we hope to give the reader an insight into the workings of the metaphysical inquiry; how debates evolve and what is at issue in them; and what kind of considerations can be used to argue for and against metaphysical claims. Our overall approach is broadly speaking a neo-Aristotelian one, and the viewpoint that we concentrate on when investigating various topics is a power ontology of a neo-Aristotelian kind that we will show can usefully be brought to bear on various debates. This is not, however, to the exclusion of different viewpoints whose merits we will also present.

SUBSTANCE

1.1 INTRODUCTION

Imagine that you are talking on the phone to a friend who has never been to your apartment. To get a better impression of what your home is like, she asks you to tell her what things there are in your living room. So you start enumerating all the things that are around you: your desk, the computer on it, your poodle Fido, your books, and so on. Listing these items seems the "right" answer to your friend's question about what there is in your living room. Yet at the same time, you could have made up quite a different list, or added some very different things to it: the smell from the curry dish you had for dinner, Fido's bark, the sunlight that comes in through the window, the brown color of your desk or the softness of Fido's ears. But to most of us, the first list will seem an intuitively more "natural" way to parse conceptually what there is in your room. And there are reasons for that. First of all, there is a way of "being in" your apartment that all the items on your initial list seem to share. Your dinner plates are there in the same way in which your books and computer are, but both are there in a different way from that in which their respective color is. Or at least so it seems, intuitively. In addition, objects such as your desk and Fido seem more "fundamental" than the desk's brown color or the softness of Fido's woolly ears, in the sense that latter ones being in your room depends in some way on the former ones being there too. Without the desk, the desk's brown color would not be in your room, either. But not the other way around: the desk would still be there, even if you painted it blue.

On a traditional view in philosophy, the material objects on your first list are thought to be "substances" and a different type of thing from the properties which they bear (such as their color, size, or texture). The Latin word *substantia*, from which the English "substance" derives, literally means "that which stands under," or supports something else: substances "support" other entities that ontologically somehow depend on them. Of course, there are many different ways in which one thing can depend on another. In a sense, a desk depends on its parts—its legs, top, and so on—and these parts in turn depend on smaller parts, down to the atoms that make up things. Such atoms are more basic than the desk—in the sense that they are the stuff of which the latter, and presumably all material objects, are made up. There is a sense of "substance" that corresponds to that of "basic stuff" that makes up things; this was the sense in which, for instance, Thales famously thought that the substance of all things was water. On an alternative understanding of ontological dependence (and correspondingly, independence), you may think that a substance is an entity that can exist "on its own" and needs no other entity to exist.[1] Whether any material objects and even atoms qualify as substances in this sense is highly questionable; perhaps nothing in the physical world does. Only

---

1. Réné Descartes for instance proposed such a view of substance in Article 51 of the first part of his *Principles of Philosophy*.

God may be a true substance in this sense, that is, something on which everything else depends, but that does not, in turn, depend on anything else.[2]

None of these two senses of "substance" is the one in which your desk, your computer, and Fido are substances, though. These items are substances in the sense of being individual particular objects, which are bearers of properties that depend on them. The idea that properties cannot just "float around" freely in the world, but need some underlying entity which bears them, or in which they "inhere",—just as a predicate in a sentence needs some grammatical subject it is predicated of—has been enormously influential in the history of philosophy. Consider for instance the following passage from John Locke, which, despite Locke's own misgivings about the traditional notion of substance, openly pays homage to it:

> The Idea . . . to which we give the general name Substance, being nothing, but the supposed, but unknown support of those Qualities we find existing, which we imagine cannot subsist, *sine re substante*, without something to support them. (*Essay Concerning Human Understanding* II, ch. 23, § 2)

What does it mean that "those Qualities we find existing" need some underlying entity "to support them"? The precise meaning of this claim depends on our understanding of what properties are; without, as yet, going into any details here, it is important to distinguish between two different theoretical options. When we normally talk of qualities and properties

2. Philosophers like Baruch Spinoza claimed that God was the only substance.

we do so as if they can be shared by different objects; we speak, for example of the brown color of your desk's top as if it is the very same color as the one your chair has. In addition to—or even as an alternative to—such "common" properties which can be shared by different objects, many philosophers think there are (also) "particular" properties of particular objects (so-called tropes), which can only be possessed by one object and cannot be shared between objects. On this view the brown color *of your desk* is a property that only your desk can have; another object might have a qualitatively similar property, but not the (numerically) very same one. Not everyone thinks that the idea of tropes makes sense; we will come back to this issue later in this chapter. But just assume, for the moment, that there are not only "common" but also "particular" properties. Locke's statement of the idea that properties "need" substances, in the passage quoted here, will then need to be formulated in a different way for each kind of property in question, the common and the particular ones. Particular properties, assuming that they exist at all, cannot exist without a particular object that supports them—for they are precisely properties of particular objects. The brown color of your desk, understood as a particular property, would not exist if your desk did not exist in the first place.

For common properties, the issue is less clear: it is famously disputed whether such properties can exist independently of any bearer. Platonists who believe in the existence of so-called transcendent universals will assume they can exist *ante res*, that is, even in the absence of anything which instantiates them. The universal Red would exist, on this view, even if there were no red objects in the world. Aristotelians disagree: they hold that universals can only exist *in rebus*. To use a neutral formulation which covers both common and particular properties, we will say that without substances there would be no properties *in the world* (because either there would not exist any properties, or, at least, they wouldn't be instantiated in the world). This was indeed, roughly put, Aristotle's view with regard to what he called "primary substances" (which correspond, more or less, to our third sense of substance, i.e., substances as individual objects). As Aristotle argued at the beginning of the *Categories*, everything that was not a primary substance itself existed only "in" a substance. (For more on Aristotle's view, see section 1.4.)

Substances are therefore widely held to be needed to "anchor" properties—either by providing the basis for their existence, or by being necessary for their instantiation in the world. The same kind of reasoning applies, *mutatis mutandis*, to relations, which are not possessed by individual objects taken singly, but which "connect" different things. "Being higher than" is not a property that your chair, for example, could have on its own when it is higher than your table. It is, instead, a relation that can only be coinstantiated by two objects, such as your chair and your table, when the first is higher than the second. Relations would need the same kind of "anchor" in the world as properties, which, again, would have to be provided by substances, such as your table and your chair. This parallel way in which substances are traditionally thought to "underlie" both properties and relations is hardly surprising. For in both cases the distinction between different entities and their relations has been modeled on the linguistic difference between subject and predicate of a sentence and the apparent dependence of both predicates and relational terms on a grammatical subject. Not all grammatical subjects have been considered to stand for genuine substances, and, as we will see in the next section, not every predicate can be taken to stand for a genuine property. But in general, the substance/property relation has widely been taken to be the ontological analog to the grammatical subject/predicate relation in a sentence.

There is also a third category of entities which substances are thought to underlie, in quite a different way. According to another influential line of thought, substances, qua bearers of properties and relations, are what underlies qualitative changes. In order to be capable of underlying changes, substances must meet at least two conditions. First, they must be capable of persisting through time. While a sudden flash of lightening is only "present" at one particular moment—it occurs at this moment, and is over immediately afterward—substances are at least generally speaking capable of persisting for some period of time. If they didn't, they couldn't underlie any changes which are noninstantaneous. For instance, your desk could not change its color from brown to blue unless it could exist for the whole stretch of time while you do the repainting. Second, substances must be capable of having contrary properties and entering into contrary relations (at least for some pairs of contraries). In order to change its color, your desk must be capable both of being brown and of not being brown, but having some other color. Not all changes can straightforwardly be understood in terms of changes in the properties or relations of "underlying" substances, though. Some changes seem to involve the coming into or going out of existence of substances themselves: for example when you build a house, a new substance (i.e., the house) comes into existence, and when the house burns down, it goes out of existence—or so it appears. Should we, in order to understand these changes in terms of the changes of properties of underlying substances, posit yet further substances which underlie these changes (e.g., the bricks of which the house is made, and which continue to exist throughout the completion of the house, through changes in their arrangement and combination)? This is a question we will set aside here, concentrating only on those changes whereby substances are neither destroyed nor created.

The idea that substance is what underlies "mundane" changes such as that of color can already be found in Aristotle, but in order to see the enormous influence of this idea, it is useful to quote someone who was highly skeptical about the notion of substance, namely David Hume, who wrote:

> When we compare [an object's] situation after a considerable change . . . and consequently . . . are presented with the idea of diversity: In order to reconcile which contradictions, the imagination is apt to feign something unknown and invisible, which it supposes to continue the same under all these variations; and this unintelligible something it calls a *substance*. (*Treatise of Human Nature*, 220)

Substances have yet a further characteristic, though, which Aristotle stressed too, and which is brought out more clearly by the Greek term that is usually translated as "substance": *ousia*. Individual substances are not just *any arbitrary* compounds or collections of things. For example, the small heap of dust on your doorstep, or the pile of philosophy books that fell from your bookshelf yesterday, are not substances. Instead, individual substances have a principle of unity that holds them together, and allows us to distinguish them from their surroundings and to say what "belongs to" a particular substance and what doesn't. Mere heaps of objects lack such a unity: you call the pile of philosophy books on your floor "*one* pile" only because the books lie on top of or next to each other, that is, on account of their physical contiguity and spatial relations. But you could also take half of those books on the floor to form a pile on their own, and talk of the books now as *two* adjacent piles of books. Whether you talk of them as one or two piles is ultimately arbitrary. If you look at a living cell, by contrast, it is not similarly "up to you" whether you call that organic material one cell or two adjacent ones. For each cell is unified by a functional principle: it needs certain parts in order to live, and only consists of the parts which are necessary for its survival and propagation, such that you cannot draw the boundaries of the cell in such a way that necessary parts are excluded.

The unifying principle which makes a substance one, unifies the substance at a particular time, but also diachronically; that is, it determines whether a substance still continues to exist as numerically the same substance over time. For instance, the living cell can continue to exist as the same cell even if significant amounts of matter constituting the cell are substituted by other matter, as it happens all the time in metabolism. (Remember, diachronic persistence of substances is important for them to be capable of underlying changes.)

Where do these unifying principles come from? According to the traditional Aristotelian view, they derive from the substance's nature or essence, which determines *what kind of being it is*. The essence of a substance (to which we will return later at more length) comprises (in first approximation) those properties without which the individual substance could no longer be what it is nor continue to exist.[3]

---

3. As we will see in chapter 3, not all properties necessarily possessed by an

Note that not all properties are like that: some properties you could acquire and lose, while staying the same substance as before, such as the property of being pale, or being tanned, and so on. Assume, by contrast, that your essence includes that you are a rational and conscious animal. If you were to completely lose your rationality or consciousness, you could then no longer exist as the particular individual you are. And, it is crucial to note, this does not just mean that you could no longer exist as a rational being, while continuing to exist as another kind of being: *you* would cease to exist at all.

We can thus sum up four key features traditionally ascribed to substances in the sense of individual particular objects as follows:

    i) Substances are bearers of properties, and of relations, which ontologically depend on them.

    ii) They underlie at least paradigmatic forms of qualitative change and are what remains the same during a change.

    iii) They are relatively stable insofar as they can exist for longer periods of time and can take on contrary properties.

    iv) They come as certain kinds of objects, having a nature that determines the kind of object they are and the conditions for their individuation at one time as well as for their diachronic persistence.

(There is a further feature usually ascribed to substances, namely that they are particulars, rather than universals,

---

existing substance are parts of its essence. However, we will set aside this complication for the time being.

which can be "shared" by different things, like properties. We have to postpone discussion of this fifth feature until the next two sections, when we discuss the relationship between substances and properties.)

Our list leaves it quite open which kinds of substances there are: for example, whether only material beings, or beings in space-time, can be substances; or whether there can be immaterial and eternal ones as well, such as God. But this is how it should be: the basic metaphysical framework we operate with should not prejudge what things there are.

Many philosophers have thought that there is an important class of entities that possess all these four features i)–iv); but many others have been skeptical, and have even doubted the coherence of these four ideas. It will be helpful to briefly consider at least one fundamental kind of worry which the set of claims i)—iv) can raise, because this concern has resurfaced in different forms again and again in the history of metaphysics.

Feature (i), that substances "underlie" properties, suggests that there is an asymmetrical relation between the two of them: properties ontologically depend on substances, but not the other way round. Does this mean that we can "remove" its properties from a substance, and the substance will nevertheless continue to exist? Imagine "peeling off" from the substance all its properties; the remainder would be a "bare particular" or "*substratum*", with *no* properties of its own. It is not clear whether we can even make sense of this idea of a bare *substratum*; for, given that such a *substratum* has no properties, it cannot be described in any way. So how could we ever get any grasp on it? Furthermore, a bare *substratum* would not have any essence or nature, and would thus fail to meet condition (iv). Nor could a substance continue to exist if it lost its essential properties. This suggests that, at least for some properties, the dependence between substances and properties must be mutual. But how does this square with feature (i)?

Many of the questions we will be concerned with in the later sections of this chapter are directly connected to this worry. In section 1.3 we will contrast the "bare particular" view of substances with its "radical" opposite, which takes substances to be mere bundles of properties. Both views face major and arguably insurmountable obstacles. However, as we will see in 1.4, there is at least one influential alternative, provided by Aristotelian hylomorphism, that allows us both to deny that substances are "bare *substrata*" of properties, and to see in which way the existence of "primary" substances is inseparable from the instantiation of the properties that comprise their individual form. We will conclude the chapter by considering an important controversy concerning the way in which substances continue to exist through time, whose resolution is crucial to understanding how substances can do the job of underlying change. Before we can go into these questions, however, we must take a brief look at the other main category we have introduced as the main counterpart to substances, namely properties.

1.2 SUBSTANCE *VERSUS* PROPERTIES

Until now we have been liberally talking about properties or qualities in order to set out what kind of roles substances are meant to play. But what are properties? A natural way to answer this question—albeit a somewhat naïve one—would be to say that a property is what a meaningful predicate expresses. Whenever we can sensibly predicate "being P" of an object A, on that view, there must be a corresponding property P which object A has to possess in order for the statement "A is P" to be true. However, the hypothesis that every meaningful predicate expresses a property leads to a famous paradox whose discovery was due to Bertrand Russell. Take the predicate "cannot be predicated of itself" (or "is not self-predicable"), which is a meaningful predicate. If that predicate denotes a property, it arguably denotes the (higher-order) property of "being non-self-predicable (or non-self-instantiating)", which is possessed by all and only those properties which cannot be predicated of themselves (or which do not instantiate themselves). For example, it will be possessed by the property of "being red," since the property of being red is not red itself. By contrast, it will not be possessed by the property "being a property," since the property of being a property is itself a property.

Let us now ask whether this property of "being non-self-predicable" is itself self-predicable or not (i.e., whether it instantiates itself or not), which must be a legitimate question to ask, if the property in question exists. If the property is self-predicable, this would mean that it is not self-predicable after all, since, in order to be self-predicable, it must be true that the property *cannot* be predicated of itself. So, the assumption that the property is self-predicable leads to a contradiction, and must be rejected. But, *pari passu*, if the property is not self-predicable, it follows that it is self-predicable after all, since "being not self-predicable" applies to all properties which cannot be predicated of themselves. So, it turns out that on the second assumption too, we arrive at a contradiction, and that the property of "being non-self-predicable" can neither be self-predicable nor non-self-predicable. So, there cannot be a genuine property of "being non-self-predicable", after all, since once we assume that there is such a property, we are led to a contradiction. And this shows that the assumption that every meaningful predicate denotes a property leads to a contradiction and cannot be sustained.

Nonetheless, we should still acknowledge that there is *some* important connection between meaningful predicates and properties, if only because such a connection is presupposed by our ordinary ways of talking about properties. The most natural way of talking about a property is to turn a predicate into a single term that can be used to refer to a property, by taking the predicate, for instance "is *F*;" strip it of the copula; and insert the prefix "the property of being . . ." to what remains. This way, one can form the nominal phrase "the property of being F"—for instance, "the property of being red," "the property of being a mile away from the center of London," and "the property of being nonself-predicable."

The connection between predicates and properties already gives us the resources to draw a rough-and-ready distinction between properties and substances, since the latter, it is usually thought, are typically referred to by grammatical subjects. Even though not all meaningful predicates correspond to properties, every property corresponds to (at least) *some* meaningful predicate or other, while substances correspond to grammatical subjects (and to them only). But is the supposedly metaphysical distinction between properties and substances *just* a reflection of this grammatical distinction? If so, it might seem that the distinction is a purely conventional one that merely reflects the contingent peculiarities of (many) natural languages. Not all philosophers would be unwilling to accept this consequence; in particular logical positivists, following Rudolf Carnap, were happy to regard all metaphysical distinctions as a matter of convention, to be assessed for their value by pragmatic considerations, especially with regard to their fruitful use in explanatory practices in the sciences. On this view, whether we can distinguish between properties and substances in our ontology is, ultimately, a question of whether our best scientific explanations and descriptions of the world have a use for this distinction, and there is no further issue "about how the world really is" at issue here. Most philosophers, by contrast, have thought that at least the property-substance distinction has a deeper metaphysical justification which goes beyond a merely pragmatic one. What could this justification be?

One way to find out is to ask which overarching ontological categories substances and properties belong to, respectively—assuming they exist. Substances in the sense of "primary substances" (i.e., the sense we have mainly been interested in in section 1.1) are particulars. Particulars are non-repeatable objects which only exist once at a time and cannot be multiply present in different things. For example, there was only one particular Napoleon Bonaparte in 1810, even though there may have been other people very similar to him, and even though the very same Napoleon might be reborn at some later point in time. But in 1810, even if there had been another person who was qualitatively exactly the same as Napoleon, he would still have been a different particular. How about properties? If you believe that (at least some) properties are universals, which can be shared by different objects at the same time, then you will regard properties as non-particulars. You are therefore committed to thinking that (at least those) properties belong to a different ontological category from substances—provided that we can draw a viable distinction between universals and particulars. One very promising way to draw this latter distinction is by appeal to the concept of instantiation. If we assume that universals and particulars exist, particulars instantiate universals. Universals can also instantiate other universals, namely "higher-order" universals (for instance, the property of "being white" instantiates the second-order property of "being a color"). But—and this is the crucial difference between universals and particulars—nothing can instantiate particulars. Drawing the distinction between universals and particulars in terms of instantiation in this way is not tantamount to denying that there can be universals that are not instantiated by anything. But every universal is *instantiable*— it *can* or *could* have instances; whilst no particular is.

This account of the distinction between universals and particulars excludes the existence of some universals that many philosophers would want to include in their ontology. For instance, if we assume that the property of being simultaneously both round and square exists, and that it is universal, it turns out that this universal can have no instances, given that any instance would have to be simultaneously round and square, which is impossible. The proposed distinction between universals and particulars therefore cannot allow the existence of such a universal, because, on the proposed criterion of instantiability, it would turn out to be a particular (!). But giving up on "self-contradictory" universals of this sort seems to be a low price to pay, overall.

Philosophers who believe that properties are not universals, but particulars (tropes), cannot use the suggested criterion of distinguishing properties from substances. For a trope is itself a particular item (or, as Campbell [1990, 20] has put it, a "particularized nature"). But perhaps for trope theorists there will not be a fundamental distinction between the two categories of substances and properties anyway. Indeed some philosophers have thought that positing tropes makes substances redundant in our ontology, because bundles of tropes could already do their work. We will turn to this view in the next section.

1.3 BEARERS OF PROPERTIES OR BUNDLES OF TROPES?

In section 1.1 we have seen that on a traditional understanding, the idea of a substance is meant to fit a certain job description, which comprises, in particular, four functions; that is, that substances are meant to be bearers of properties, to underlie paradigmatic forms of change, to be able to persist through time, and to have a nature and principle of (both synchronic and diachronic) unity. But as we have seen at the end of section 1.1, there are reasons to suspect that nothing can fulfill these four functions at the same time, such that the traditional notion of "substance" might turn out to be inconsistent. In this section and the next, we want to develop more explicitly this worry, putting it in terms of the relationship between a substance and its properties.

When we reflect on the relationship between substance and properties, there are two fundamentally opposed ways of construing this relationship: you can either think that substances are nothing more than the cluster of their qualities, or that they are something "over and above" such qualities. Intuitively, one might be inclined to resist the idea that a substance is more than its qualities; what would this something "extra" be, and how would we know that it is there, given that we cannot perceive it (directly, at least, since everything we can perceive directly must have some qualitative features)? If it were just a quality-less "extra," we could not describe it in any way, but at best refer to it by saying "this thing without . . ."; but don't we need to have some idea of what kind of object we are referring to even in order to do the latter? On the other hand, one reason for thinking that a substance is something more than the sum of the qualities it has, which we have already encountered in section 1.1, is that some of these properties may change (e.g., the color of an object) and yet the substance in some important sense could remain the same substance. The same *what*? Not the same set of qualities, obviously, because *ex hypothesi* at least one of the properties has changed and a set is individuated in terms of its members. What is it then that has remained the same while one or more qualities have changed? Some philosophers take the view that there is something that underlies the properties and holds them all together, and this is what remains the same when some properties are replaced. What remains is a *substratum* that is itself without any qualities (in order to be able to take on qualities of any kind). Being property-less or bare, the *substratum* cannot be perceived, but we can "reach" it via a process of abstraction. Consider, for instance, the book you are reading as an example of a substance. Mentally, you can strip away from it its colors, texture, weight, and so on, until you reach the particular but property-less *substratum* that underlies all these properties. The issue is how we can know and describe this bare *substratum*, given that it is meant to have no properties whatsoever when considered on its own. Its bareness is such that we can only say of it that it exists. But if so, how can it be anything at all? The difficulty of addressing this question makes many feel that the *substratum* is a sort of mysterious entity that we would better do without in our ontology. (Remember Hume's mockery of the "unknown and invisible" item, which we quoted in section 1.1 as a forceful expression of such doubts.)

If one is suspicious of the idea of a bare particular as bearer of properties, one might be attracted by the opposite, equally radical, solution. Just as a bare particular is supposed to be something without properties, could we not equally well do away with substances as particulars, and think of substances as nothing over and above the sets of their properties? On this view, there is nothing more to a particular substance than the properties that qualify it. Even though it is so radical, there is something to be said in favor of this solution: for if there is no remainder once all the properties have been removed, then we have at least some reason to think that the substance we are examining, such as this book, cannot be more than the ensemble of those properties.

It is important to note at this point that the two theories of substance we are examining differ in terms of ontological parsimony. On the former, a substance is made up of two types of entity: the properties and the *substratum*. On the latter, a substance is made up of only one type of entity: the properties (arranged in a certain way). The second theory is thus a simpler one, insofar as it invokes fewer types of entity. There is no decisive reason why a simpler and more economical theory is more likely to be true than a complex and uneconomical one; but philosophers (and scientists) by and large place a considerable premium on the simplicity of a theory. Certainly there seems no reason to tolerate redundancy in one's theory of the world; and in our case the *substratum* is not only an apparently unnecessary addition to the ontology, but, even worse, an addition that looks mysterious and unknowable. But before we can justifiably take the view that the *substratum* is not needed in our ontology, we have to consider in more detail the theory that substances are nothing above sets of properties, and see whether it is viable in its own right. There are two variants of this latter view:

a) Substances are nothing but sets of universal properties (e.g., the universal "white");
b) Substances are nothing but sets of particular properties or tropes (e.g., "the white of this page").

On the first view, the book in your hand is a collection of the universals "white," "hard," "made from paper," et cetera; on the second a collection of the tropes "the white of this page," "the hardness of this book's cover," and so on.

Looking back at the distinction between particulars and universals we have drawn in section 1.2, we can say that variant a) tries to account for substances solely in terms of universals (i.e., items which are shareable by different objects), without any additional "particular" element. The apparent particularity of substances is meant to be explained in terms of shareable properties. This accords well with the main motivation for the bundle theory: while we seem to have a good grasp on the qualities of objects, bundle theorists find it hard to make sense of the idea that there is something which is devoid of such qualities, but merely a "this." And particularity, unless it can be explained away, threatens to lead us to a quality-less "this." But will such an explanation work; or is our understanding of substances too much wedded to their being particulars to allow for an understanding of substances merely in terms of items which are universal rather than particular?

The main objection to variant a) is the following: if every object is a set of universal properties, two numerically distinct objects x and y that possesses exactly the same properties must be the same substance (thus, (a) commits us to the identity of qualitatively indiscernible objects). But this contradicts our initial assumption that x and y were numerically different. And it doesn't seem intuitively plausible that two qualitatively identical objects could not be numerically different.

In reply, one might want to say that there is a principled reason why two distinct substances could not share all their properties: because they must (at least) have different spatiotemporal locations. Assuming that no two entirely distinct substances can occupy the same space at the same time, it seems that each object will bear a unique set of properties, after all. There is a first, obvious drawback to this proposal, in that it only allows for distinct substances with the same properties when these substances are spatially located. Even if you believe that de facto all existing substances are in space, you might worry that, at least in principle, there could be other substances as well which you might want to distinguish numerically even if they have the same properties (e.g., two qualitatively identical angels). There is, however, an even deeper problem with the proposal: there is no guarantee that distinct things will have different properties, unless we reintroduce some "particular" (non-repeatable) element into our metaphysics. Here is why. Should we think of position in space (and time) as an absolute, or relative matter? If absolute, this would suggest that there is some kind of particularity to spatial positions. A position would be a particular, a non-repeatable point in space. (Just think of a Cartesian coordinate system, where the points are uniquely identified by their coordinates: these points *are* particulars that cannot recur.) But this means that the notion of a particular—one that is not defined as a bundle of qualities—will have come back into our theory. This is a major drawback, since proposal a) wanted to provide an understanding of substances *without* reference to particulars; and even worse, the kind of particularity that has "sneaked back" into our system is one we understand even less than the original particularity of substances. So should we instead define spatial positions in relation to each other? The problem with doing so is that there is at least the possibility that the space of a universe has a "line of symmetry", such that places in corresponding positions on either side of the line of symmetry would bear an identical set of relations to all the other places within the whole of that space. Imagine a universe that consists solely of two otherwise qualitatively identical spheres, that are placed at equal distance on either side of our imaginary line of symmetry. These two spheres would have all their non-relational and relational properties alike, and we could distinguish them neither by the properties they have "considered on their own" (i.e., their intrinsic properties) nor by their relational properties—a possibility that Max Black (1952) presented vividly in a famous thought experiment. On the first version of the bundle theory, they will therefore again collapse into one another—but *ex hypothesi* the two spheres are numerically distinct.

So, defenders of version a) of the bundle theory will find it hard to avoid the implication that particulars with all the same properties collapse into one. Thus, they have major difficulties in accounting for our strong intuition that, for substances, numerical identity and qualitative identity are not the same thing. Let us turn to the second version of the bundle theory, b), to examine whether it does any better on that count. The objection, that the theory entails that bundles with all the same properties must be one and the same, has "bite" only if properties are understood in a certain way: as shareable and repeatable items fundamentally different from particulars. Perhaps, though, properties are particularized in some way, as trope theory suggests. In this case, the black in the bundle of properties corresponding to this laptop would be a different item from the black in another bundle of properties which corresponds to another substance. If properties are conceived of as tropes, that is as particular properties, then the problem of the numerical distinctness of qualitatively identical substances will not arise, since no particular property could be a member of two different bundles and no two different bundles could have exactly the same members.

The most obvious problem with this variant of the bundle theory is how to explain the similarity between different tropes and between bundles. We couldn't say that this page of the book has the same color as another one, since each page has its specific particular color that is different from the color of every other page. And even if this problem could somehow be resolved, there would remain a yet deeper worry, namely that version b) could save the bundle theory only at the cost of failing to do justice to the theory's underlying motivation. The main aim of the bundle theory, we saw, was to account for substances entirely in terms of properties. The particularity of substances was meant to be "explained away" in terms of coinstantiated properties. Now it seems that we are able to salvage the bundle theory from the objection that two identical bundles would collapse into one, only if we understand properties in some way as particulars. For in order to make the bundles of properties behave more like the particulars that we take objects to be, we had to make our properties look like particulars. Particularity has therefore "sneaked back" into our theory again.

There are yet further difficulties for the view that substances are bundles of properties, which concern in particular the question of whether on this view substances could fulfill the "job description" for substances we encountered in the set of characteristics i) to iv) in section 1.1. These difficulties apply to any version of the bundle theory, whether one thinks that properties are universal or particular; and concern e.g. the question of how the theory accounts for change in objects. If a substance were just a collection of properties, then strictly speaking it couldn't survive any change. If one property was lost and another gained, we would have a different collection of properties, on the assumption that what makes a collection the same thing at different times is that it is composed of the same component items. Consequently, two collections are different if the things collected within them are different. However, the particulars that interest us change (qualitatively) all the time, while remaining (numerically) the same. The point will become intuitively clear if we consider a human being as an exemplary substance. A human being changes radically from childhood to adulthood. How could a person be just a collection of properties when her/his properties change all the time?

The bundle view of substances seems therefore hardly tenable. For ultimately, the idea that substances are particular individuals cannot be explained just in terms of their having certain qualities—either these qualities will be shareable and thus will not ensure particularity, or else they will themselves be primitively particularized and thus cannot be used *to account for* particularity. Does this mean that we are compelled to opt for the alternative to the bundle theory, that is, the *substratum* view? We are not; and this is good news, given the existing worries about the intelligibility of the *substratum* view. For there are theories of substance that hold that substances are different from bare particulars, though different from mere collections of properties. The most influential such theory is Aristotle's hylomorphism, which we will consider in the next section. In doing so, we will not only see whether Aristotle can make sense of substances' being particular objects; we will also examine to what extent Aristotle's theory succeeds in addressing the worry that we encountered at the end of section 1.1.

1.4 ARISTOTLE'S HYLOMORPHISM

In the *Metaphysics* Aristotle puts forward his well-known theory of substance, known as *hylomorphism*, according to which substances are "compounds" of matter (*hyle*) and form (*morphe*). The form is the principle of unity and of functional organization of the substance—which determines the *kind of thing* that the object is. Matter is the substratum in which such a principle is implemented; for instance flesh and bones for a human being, or marble for a statue. Aristotle's hylomorphic analysis applies to all substances, those which are artificially produced as well as natural ones. Even the soul–body relationship is, for Aristotle, to be understood in these terms: the soul is the substantial form of an organic body, and the body is the matter of the soul, just as the ball-shape of an elastic ball is the latter's form, while the bouncy stuff it is made of is its matter. Forms are universal, and as such the numerically same form can be instantiated in multiple parcels of matters at the same time; while the same amount of matter can take on different forms. For example, a plank of wood can be carved into a desk's top and later the desk's top can be carved into table legs. But—remember Aristotle's rejection of universals *ante rem*—forms can only exist as implemented in matter (at least in the physical sublunary world); there exist no disembodied ball-shapes and, *pari passu*, no disembodied souls for Aristotle. Conversely, there cannot exist matter that is not en-formed by some form or other. (Even a block of marble has a substantial form: it is a block.)

How do matter and form compose *one* substance, then? Most ancient and modern commentators have interpreted Aristotle's views as if the hylomorphic compound were a mereological sum (i.e., a compound which consisted of matter and form as two distinct elements, just as a multi-member set consists of distinct elements), and have then tried to understand what relationship could adequately bring together those parts into a unity. Often Aristotle has even been accused of having failed to account for the unity of substance, and his hylomorphism has been declared in need of "reconditioning."[4] We cannot give an overview of the debate here, which is very complex and has been ongoing since the ancient commentators' time. Rather, we will

4. See, e.g., Witt (1994).

give some of the crucial textual evidence that shows that the mereological approach to the unity of substance is misguided, as Aristotle did not conceive of substances in that way; we will then present one interpretation that takes a non-mereological approach.

It becomes clear that thinking of the matter and form of a substance as parts that are somehow related to each other to form a unified compound is a mistake if we look at a key text in which Aristotle presents his position: *Metaphysics*, book VII, chap. 17. In this passage, through the so-called Syllable Regress, Aristotle introduces the thesis that the form cannot unify the parts of a substance if it is itself an additional part of the substance (or a relation which holds between those parts). Aristotle starts from the example of the two letters *b* and *a* that make up the syllable *ba*, and asks what unifies the two letters into *one* syllable. If what unifies them is an additional element, says Aristotle, then the syllable would be composed of three elements: two letters and the unifying element. What would unify these three elements in a single syllable, then? If this were a further additional element, then one should ask again what unifies the first two and the new element into one syllable, and so on *ad infinitum* (*Metaphysics* VII.17, 1041b11–22). It is important to stress that from this regress, Aristotle does not draw the same negative conclusion that the British Idealist F. H. Bradley drew from his version of this regress over two thousand years later: namely, that there is no way to genuinely unify the many into one (Bradley, 1893). For Aristotle, the form of the syllable *does* unify the letters (and generalizing, the substantial form unifies matter and form); but not as an additional element; rather, as a *principle* (*Metaphysics* VII.17, 1041b25–31).

How is the form *qua* principle able to unify the substance for Aristotle? To give the reader at least a sketch of a non-mereological account of substantial unification, we will present one such interpretation of Aristotle's views. Marmodoro (2013, following Scaltsas 1994) argues that for Aristotle substances are paradigmatic unities, wherein the parts that compose them have undergone a *change in their identity criteria* by becoming parts of the substance, so they are not in it as identifiable and distinct parts in the same way they were when they were "outside of" or separate from the substance. The role of the substantial form as unifying principle of the substance is to "strip" the constituents of their original criteria of identity, and make them functionally and definitionally dependent on the substance of which they have become parts. So, what changes when the elements *b* and *a* make up the syllable *ba*? Aristotle's view becomes clearer in another passage of *Metaphysics*, where he introduces the so-called Homonymy Principle:

> [The parts of a substance] cannot even exist if severed from the whole, for it is not a finger in any state that is the finger of a living thing, but the dead finger is a finger only homonymously. (*Metaphysics* VII 10, 1035b23–25)

If the parts retained their own identity when making up a new substance, they would continue to be what they were even if separated (again) from the substance. But Aristotle claims that when severed (physically or in abstraction) from the whole, the parts of a substance cease to be what they were while constituting parts of the substance. This means that parts are identified differently when they are part of a substance and when they are separated from it. When they make up a substance, the parts gain a new identity according to the unifying principle of the substantial form. When they are separated from the substance, they lose that functional identity that is conferred on them by the substantial form: in Aristotle's example, a finger separated from a living body has no function as a finger anymore; hence it is only a finger by homonymy, that is, only in name. The Homonymy Principle explains how elements that are originally numerically distinct get unified into a single entity through their *transformation* from elements to functional parts of a substance on which they become dependent, analogously to the way in which the finger is dependent on the living body. (This point should not be misunderstood: the parts do not go out of existence when entering the composition of a substance; there remains physical continuity between, for example, the letters *a* and *b* taken separately and them as parts of the syllable *ba*; but notwithstanding physical continuity, their criteria of identity have changed when the letters have become part of the syllable.)

Let us look back at some of the questions about substance we have examined in the previous sections of this chapter. To begin with, how does Aristotle's hylomorphism allow us to solve the worry about the traditional notion of substance we have encountered at the end of section 1.1? First, a primary substance is not a bare particular, but has a substantial form or essence that makes it the kind of substance it is and provides it with its principle of unity. This substantial form is not just another property of the substance which is "instantiated" in the substance in the same way as other properties are. It is "said of" the substance in a different way from the other properties which are "inherent in" substances. Aristotle would therefore reject the idea, which provided the starting point of our worry, that all properties could be "peeled off" from the substance, because for him they are not all instantiated in it in the same way. Second, Aristotle accepts, for the properties relevant to the individual form, mutual dependence between the instantiation of these properties and the existence of the substance. So there is good reason to think that at least Aristotle succeeded in making the set of the characteristics i) and iv) a coherent one and, at the same time, in providing an account of the unity of a substance. Furthermore, since not all properties of a substance are part of its form, Aristotle has a way to account for the idea that substance underlies at least an important class of changes. For since the substance can persist as long as it maintains its form, it can persist through change in its other, accidental, properties. What about the question of the particularity of substances we have discussed in section 1.3? For Aristotle, the matter of which the substance is constituted plays a crucial role in the substance's individuation. For this matter is not, in its turn, another property that could be shared by different substances of the same kind. Rather, matter accounts for the fact that two substances may be numerically distinct even when they are qualitatively identical. Forms, for Aristotle, cannot constitute an individual substance on their own; only when they are "en-forming" an amount of matter do we have an individual substance, and in the latter the matter out of which the substance is constituted can be used to distinguish the substance from others which have the same form but are constituted out of different matter. Aristotle thus provides a comprehensive and (at least prima facie) consistent set of answers to the questions concerning substance that we have encountered so far.

This makes his view an appealing account of substance and a serious alternative to other past and present positions in metaphysics, as is shown by the renewed and ever growing interest for this theory of the past few decades.[5]

1.5 HOW DO SUBSTANCES PERSIST?

In our discussion of how the unity of substances works for Aristotle, we have mainly focused on the relation between substances and their spatial or bodily parts. But the question of the *transtemporal* unity of substances– that is, how a substance can persist through time and continue to be the same particular substance as it has been before– has been equally central to the debate about substances. Do concrete particulars and substances persist over time, and if so, how do they do it? (Remember, as we have seen in section 1.1, it is crucial that substances can persist over time if they are to "underlie" ordinary changes and thus do the work they are supposed to do.) What are the criteria of identity through time for artifacts, animals, people?

It is well know that these questions engender difficulties, the best-known of which is presented by the Ship of Theseus case. According to legend, the Athenians kept the ship with which Theseus had sailed to Crete to slay the Minotaur as a memorial. But now imagine that over the years, the ship's planks, due to their age, have to be replaced one by one. What happens to Theseus's ship if the first plank is replaced: does it remain the same? The answer seems to be yes. But if the process is continued, by parity of reasoning at each step, the ship will then remain the same even though,

5. See, e.g., Koslicki (2008), Lowe (2012), Rea (2011), Jaworski (2016).

and when, *all* its planks have been replaced. Imagine now that someone has kept all the old planks, which have been gradually replaced, and once the replacement is completed, assembles them to build a new ship out of them (which has, we can imagine, exactly the same structure and shape as Theseus's old ship). There are two ships now, but the original ship of Theseus can be numerically identical with at most one of them. Which one is it supposed to be identical with? This question raises difficult puzzles, because our intuitions about how to determine transtemporal persistence for a substance pull us in different directions here. In the Ship of Theseus case, we are torn between two intuitions: the intuition that the identity of the ship rests on its continuing functional unity, within which individual parts can be replaced; and the intuition that the ship is just assembled from its parts and its identity therefore cannot be fully divorced from the latters' identity.

We will not directly deal with criteria for transtemporal persistence for specific kinds of substances here. Rather, we will address what has become a foundational issue for these questions in much of the contemporary debate. This is the issue of whether objects have temporal parts, which has become the object of a heated controversy over the last couple of decades. What view one takes on the issue of temporal parts seems to prejudge, to a considerable degree, the answers one can give to the other questions about persistence.

When you first hear about objects' having "temporal" parts, as well as spatial or bodily parts, you may well be at a loss to imagine what could be meant by the former locution. One way that is often used to make this locution more intelligible takes as its point of departure the thought that the existence of objects and people extends through time as well as through space: you existed yesterday, and you will exist tomorrow too. Furthermore, just as you can have different properties at different places of your body (your hands are cold, while your feet are not), you can have different properties at different times (yesterday you were pale, but if you stay in the sun today, tomorrow you'll be tanned). But how do you extend through time? Some philosophers believe that you do so by having different temporal parts at different times. Your spatial parts are things like your head, your feet, and your nose; your temporal parts are things like you-yesterday, you-today, and you-tomorrow. Your being pale yesterday and being tanned tomorrow can be explained in terms of the you-yesterday part being pale, while the you-tomorrow part is tanned. Similarly, your existing yesterday and today can then be explained by the you-yesterday part existing yesterday, and the you-today part of you existing today. Other philosophers consider this view as fundamentally flawed. They argue that you persist through time as a whole: it was the very same whole person who was pale yesterday, and the very same whole person will be suntanned tomorrow. "You-yesterday" isn't a name for some mysterious part of you which only existed for a day, on this view; instead, it's a convoluted way of talking about you and what you were like yesterday.

The view that objects have temporal parts and are, in that sense, extended in time, just as they are extended in space, is called *perdurantism* (e.g., Quine 1953b; Lewis 1986a; Sider 2001). Perdurantists believe that ordinary things like animals, boats, and planets exist through time in virtue of their temporal parts existing at different times (the things persist by "perduring" through different stages). Endurantists, who deny the temporal parts view (see, e.g., Chisholm 1976; Fine

2000; Wiggins 2001), believe instead that things are wholly present whenever they exist (things persist by "enduring").

Advocates of the temporal parts view typically argue that their position solves a number of metaphysical problems. In particular, they often claim that supposing that you have temporal parts allows us to easily explain how you can have different properties at different times. This possibility, they argue, would otherwise be mysterious, since it would involve ascribing to you incompatible properties. Take the peach in your fruit bowl that was unripe a few days ago, and today is overripe. Surely nothing can be both unripe and over-ripe? Of course, it is the fact that the peach is unripe and overripe *at different times* which saves us from metaphysical trouble here: we all know that. But what precisely is it about the passage of time that makes it possible for one and the same object to have apparently incompatible properties? If the peach has temporal parts, this easily explains how it can change: an earlier temporal part of the peach is unripe, while a later temporal part of the peach is overripe, and we are all familiar with the fact that different parts of the same object can have different properties (just as your hands can be cold, while your feet are warm). But we should note that this solution, which is meant to explain the possibility of qualitative changes in substances, strictly speaking doesn't allow for this possibility. Change, for the perdurantists, involves the succession of one part after another, but one and the very same item—one part—never changes its properties. What changes its properties is only the whole, which changes them derivatively, by courtesy of the succession of its parts.

Endurantists have offered their own explanations to the phenomenon of change. Some endurantists embrace presentism, the view that only present objects, events, and states exist: past and future do not exist. Presentism seems to dissolve the problem of change: since only the overripe peach is present, its unripe state does not exist, so there's nothing to worry about, because there are no *prima facie* inconsistent states of the peach which would have to be reconciled. Other endurantists claim that objects change by standing in different relations to different times. There is no absolute "timeless" fact of the matter regarding the ripeness of the peach: instead, the peach bears the *being-unripe-on* relation to Monday, and the *being-overripe-on* relation to Friday. Yet a third endurantist option is to advocate adverbialism. Change is puzzling because it seems that one and the same object (the peach) both has and doesn't have a single property (like "being-unripe"). The adverbialist idea is that instead of subdividing the object into temporal parts (the peach-on-Monday and the peach-on-Friday), or subdividing the property (into "being-unripe-on-Monday" and "being-unripe-on-Friday"), we should distinguish the ways in which the object has the property. We draw such distinctions in many other respects too, which have nothing to do with temporality; for example, the peach can have the property of "being overripe" in a mild or an extreme way (depending on how overripe it is). Similarly, according to the adverbialist proposal, the peach has the property "being-unripe" in a "Monday"-way, and it fails to have that same property in a "Friday"-way. Again, this would escape the contradiction worry, since there is no problem about something being F in one way, without being F in another way: your walk to the library yesterday could have been a slow walk, without being an elegant walk.

Hence, we can conclude that assuming temporal parts is not necessary to explain the possibility of change in properties of a substance. Moreover, if Aristotle's considerations on the unity of substance presented in the last section are correct, assuming temporal parts leads to a different problem: the problem of explaining how those parts form a unified substance. This explanation cannot be the same as when we ask how different bodily parts form a unified substance. For in the latter case, the parts which are being unified already exist (even though, as we have seen, according to one interpretation of Aristotle, not as the same objects as they would be if separated from the substances), and the same holds for the matter out of which the substance is made. By contrast, when temporal parts of a substance are unified into one, not all these parts will already be in existence, at least not when the substance still exists or is still alive, for then many temporal parts will still be future, not-yet existing ones. How can these non-existing parts be unified to those already past or present to form one temporally extended substance?

This difficulty for the perdurantist, added to the fact that it is unnecessary to embrace perdurantism in order to account for the possibility of change in a substance's properties, already weighs strongly against this position. But there is a further consideration, which has to be taken into account not only when deciding the issue between perdurantism and endurantism, but also for other contexts. Perdurantism certainly goes against many of our pretheoretical intuitions about substances and their existence through time. We do not normally believe that a substance is only present "in part" at a certain point of time, but that it is wholly so. This distinguishes, according to our ordinary line of thought, the substance from its history or "biography" which is only partially present at one time (unless the substance is extremely short-lived, of course). Endurantists capture the former intuition, and maintain the latter distinction, while perdurantists don't, and the latter require, to this extent, a much more drastic revision of our pretheoretical views. Of course, the fact that a philosophical theory asks for such a revision is not, *per se,* a clinching argument against it. But if such a revision is not needed in order to account for certain other phenomena we are committed to (in our case: the possibility of change in the property of a substance) and does not bring any other significant advantages over its less revisionary rivals, the departure from our pretheoretical views does seem to speak against a theory. In the light of this additional consideration, it seems decidedly preferable to us to espouse endurantism, especially if one finds the story about the unity of substances presented in 1.4. to be along the right lines. There is strong reason to suspect that perdurantists have mixed up two things: the substance, and its history or "biography." The second does have temporal parts—but that doesn't mean that the first has, too.

1.6 CONCLUSIONS

In this chapter we have introduced a key concept of traditional and contemporary metaphysics, that of substance. We examined the considerations that make us posit substances as particular and individual beings. We also introduced some of the recurring philosophical issues concerning substance; the distinction between substance and properties; the unity of substance; and the issue of the temporal persistence of substance. We looked at the theoretical functions that a concept such as that of substance has to fulfill and which constrain which metaphysical theories of substance can be plausible. In doing so, we have become acquainted with some of the key considerations metaphysicians appeal to in deciding between rival theories (such as considerations of ontological parsimony, and to what extent a theory requires revision of our pretheoretical intuitions). As we will see, many of these issues, and many of these philosophical "moves," will come up again in the next chapter, which is about properties.

*

PROPERTIES AND

RELATIONS

2.1 INTRODUCTION

In this chapter we will discuss properties, such as being red, being circular, being fragile, and so on. We will start with the issue of whether properties are entities that should be included in our ontology in addition to substances, or whether they are merely ways substances are, and thus should not be regarded as "extra" entities in our ontology (section 2.2). We will then introduce a set of related issues concerning fundamentality, reduction, and eliminativism, which will serve as the theoretical framework within which to think about the status of properties in the ontology (section 2.3). Afterwards, we will proceed to distinguish the dispositional properties, or *powers*, of an object (e.g., being elastic) from its categorical properties (e.g., being spherical) and will discuss why many contemporary metaphysicians are still skeptical about the existence of the former (sections 2.4 and 2.5). Many, however, have not only come to enthusiastically embrace powers as properties in their own right, but have gone so far as to maintain that *all* properties are powers, or that powers are the building blocks from which everything else derives; we will introduce and discuss this view in section 2.6. Finally, we will address the issue of whether relations too are to be added to our ontology, in addition to monadic properties and substances (section 2.7). While presenting arguments from both sides of the debate concerning properties and relations, we will encourage the reader to assess them for herself in terms of soundness and cogency and take a stance of her own.

2.2 DO PROPERTIES EXIST? REALISM *VERSUS* NOMINALISM

One of the most well-known disputes in the history of metaphysics concerns the existence of properties as entities in their own right. With respect to substances, it is very hard to deny that at least some particular substances exist as entities in their own right. You, for instance, and Fido and all the things in your room, seem to be entities whose existence is beyond doubt (unless you are a skeptic about the external world). We might doubt the existence of certain classes of substances (e.g., of ghosts or the oases you see in the desert after an exhausting walk under the sun), but surely some particular substances exist. Properties are a different matter. Why should we posit the existence of properties, as entities in their own right, over and above the existence of the particular substances which possess these properties? The traditional debate about this question has been between "realists" and "nominalists." The latter deny that there are universal properties to which general terms (*nomina*), which we use to talk about how things are, refer. Realists have argued in response that we have to admit properties into our ontology, because they have important explanatory work to do. In particular, realists have argued that properties serve four main explanatory functions.[1]

First, consider the sentence "Fido is white." The expression "Fido" refers to a particular object: your poodle Fido. What does the predicate expression "is white" refer to? Does it not also have to refer to something in order to have meaning, and in order for the whole sentence to make sense? If so, it seems, the property *being white* must exist for the predicate "is white" to refer to. Second, assume that the sentence "Fido is white" is true. What makes it true, or accounts for its being true? It cannot be just Fido on his own (after all, Fido might have another color and still be Fido). Rather, at least on one influential view in the debate, what accounts for the truth of that sentence is that Fido instantiates the property of being white. On this view, we have three things that explain why the sentence is true: (i) Fido, (ii) the property of being white, and (iii) that Fido instantiates this property. But this explanation only works if the property of being white exists alongside Fido (for the relation of instantiation can only hold between things that exist). Third, compare Fido, who is white, and you newly bought t-shirt that is white too. (We will assume here, to make matters easier, that Fido and your t-shirt have exactly the same shade and tone of white.) Fido and your t-shirt have something in common, on account of their both being white—there is something that they share. The most straightforward explanation for this, or so it seems, is that there is one common property that they both share— that is, the general property of being white. Fourthly, some philosophers hold that we need to posit that properties exist

---

1. For the first three cf. Rapp (2016, 46f).

if we want to take seriously scientific practice in the natural sciences. What scientists are trying to find out are natural laws that hold universally. These laws, some philosophers have argued (most prominently David Armstrong), are best thought of as connecting universal properties (e.g., Einstein's relativity formula $E=mc^2$ is best interpreted as connecting general properties such as having a certain mass and energy).

These are four key explanatory functions that properties are widely held to fulfill in metaphysics. How do they relate to the distinction we drew in chapter 1 (section 1.1) between universal and particular properties? Not all the four arguments advanced in support of the existence of properties as entities in their own right work equally well on both conceptions of properties. The first two arguments go through on both conceptions of properties; but the last two are successful only on the assumption that properties are understood as universals, that is, as properties that different substances can share. With regard to the fourth argument, this is immediately obvious, since the argument is directly formulated in terms of universal properties. The third argument too presupposes that properties are conceived of as universals. For if properties were tropes, then the whiteness of Fido and the whiteness of your t-shirt would not be the same entity. As a result, that both Fido and your t-shirt have a whiteness trope among their properties could not mean that they have literally something in common, and thus does not *explain* their similarity. (This is a difficulty we will return to later in this section.)

How convincing are these four arguments in support of the existence of properties as entities in their own right? The first argument relies explicitly on the idea that linguistic expressions must refer to something or other in order to have meaning. Philosophers by and large consider this assumption unconvincing. It rests on the extension to all linguistic expressions of a model which has at least some *prima facie* plausibility in the case of names and singular terms. In the case of the name "Fido," it is plausible to think the name gets its meaning from the object it stands for, or denotes (i.e., your poodle). Or to put the point slightly more cautiously: it is plausible to think that its meaning is *at least partly* determined by the object the name stands for. If "Fido" was not the name of your poodle, but of your cat, then the expression "Fido" would have a different meaning from the one it actually has. But even if we accepted this picture for the case of proper names and singular terms, what reason would there be to assume that all linguistic expressions must function in that way? Philosophers like Ludwig Wittgenstein have put forward powerful arguments to show that this assumption is fallacious, and that it neglects the many different functions linguistic expressions can have. With an apt phrasing, Gilbert Ryle has called the idea that all expressions get their meaning by denoting an entity, the " 'Fido'–Fido" fallacy: just as we think that "Fido" stands for Fido, "is white" must stand for an object as well.[2] But this *is* a fallacy. Even for proper names and singular terms it is not at all clear that their having a meaning depends on their "standing for" an object. Just think of the names for fictional characters we use, such as "Pegasus." These names have a meaning. If you know some Greek mythology, you will know what "Pegasus" means. But how could there be an object this term stands for, since

2. See Ryle (1949, 70).

Pegasus doesn't exist?[3] Thus, the first argument for positing the existence of properties as entities in their own right for explanatory reasons seems to be unsound.

How about the second argument, namely that properties are needed to explain what makes a sentence true? This argument raises two main worries. Let us consider them in turn. To begin with, one can ask whether the existence of properties is genuinely needed to explain the truth of a sentence like "Fido is white." Thinking that there is a property of whiteness which Fido instantiates may be one way of explaining the statement's truth, but there may be alternative ways, too. For instance, it might be a brute fact about Fido—that is, his being white—that makes the sentence "Fido is white" true, and this fact may require or admit of no further explanation. Or, a nominalist could argue that our particular Fido on his own *is enough* to explain what makes the sentence "Fido is white" true. For, after all, our Fido *is* white (even if he might have had another color). So, Fido on his own is *ipso facto* a white dog. What more is needed to explain the truth of "Fido is white"? Furthermore, one can reasonably be skeptical about whether the explanation of the truth of "Fido is white" in terms of Fido's instantiation of the property "being white" is a satisfactory, or even viable account at all. Remember that according to this account there are three things which explain why the sentence is true: (i) Fido, (ii) the property of being white, and (iii) that Fido instantiates this property. Now consider (iii) and ask

3. Perhaps you still feel attracted to the idea that there must be some object, perhaps a *non-existent* Pegasus, to which " 'Pegasus' " refers, given that the term " 'Pegasus' " is meaningful. If you do, you will have sympathies for a Meinongian position, which accepts non-existent objects in its ontology. But we will not go into this latter philosophical view here.

yourself: what makes it the case that "Fido instantiates the property of being white" is true? The only difference between this sentence and our original one "Fido is white" is, it seems, that our new sentence includes a two-place relational predicate rather than a monadic one. But let us ignore this distinction for the moment, since, if an explanation is needed for what makes sentences involving monadic predicates true, we need just as much an explanation for what makes sentences involving relational predicates true. And, if we found a good answer to the first question, we would expect it applies to the second question as well. Let us then try to apply the proposed solution to the question of what makes "Fido instantiates the property of being white" true. Just as in our original case it was the property of "being white," in this case it is the relation of "instantiating," which we must posit along with Fido and the property of being white. But in addition to that, it seems, we must also assume that Fido and the property of being white instantiate jointly the instantiation relation. And this seems to lead us directly to an infinite regress, since the move we just made can be repeated at the next level as well. In order to explain what makes the original statement "Fido is white" true, we must now posit an infinite number of instantiation relations which hold between Fido, the property of being white, the instantiation relation, et cetera. How bad is this? Our assessment of this outcome will depend on some further issues. For instance, if you think that a relation cannot instantiate itself, and therefore the instantiation relation at each level must be a different one from the one introduced at the preceding level, then you will consider the resulting infinite regress as particularly problematic. The regress will then involve not just an infinity of instantiations of the instantiation relation, but an infinity of different relations, too (instantiation, meta-instantiation, meta-meta-instantiation, etc.)—which would be a hard bullet to bite. Alternatively, one might try to stop the regress by claiming that at the second level, the question of what makes it true that Fido instantiates the property of being white does not arise. But why not? Is stopping the regress here not an arbitrary move? And if we can claim that the question of what makes the sentence true does not arise at the second level, can we not do so already on the first level, and thus block the original argument for the existence of properties? As a consequence, the second argument in support of positing the existence of properties as entities in their own right doesn't look too promising either.

Things are different when we come to the third argument, though, (namely, that Fido and your t-shirt have something in common by virtue of both being white) and even many nominalists have conceded that this argument has some force. To respond to it, some nominalists have attempted to provide an account of the (intuitive) starting point of the argument that doesn't rely on the existence of universal properties shared by Fido and your t-shirt. There are ways to argue that both Fido and your t-shirt do have something in common even if there are no universal properties: they have something in common in that they belong to one class of objects (i.e., the class of all white things). But to this, one may reply that shared membership in one class does not in fact capture what Fido and your t-shirt have in common, that is, their color. Classes are individuated by their members: two classes are identical if and only if they have all their members in common. Now suppose that two different properties F and G "go together"—either de facto or even necessarily; for example the property of having a surface,

F, and the property of having a color, G. Then the classes of things with a surface and of things that have a color will have the same members, and, as a result, be identical. But, *ex hypothesi*, the two properties F and G were different. Belonging to the same class of objects thus is not the same as having the same property. Alternatively, nominalists have tried to explain that two white objects have something in common in terms of resemblance or similarity: two white objects seem to have something in common because they resemble one another (which does not require that there is literally something that both objects share). However, this proposal too runs into difficulties. On the one hand, objects can be similar and dissimilar in different respects. Fido can be similar to your t-shirt in respect of color, but very dissimilar from it with respect to his size and ability to move around. So, it seems that we cannot do justice to the intuition that Fido and your t-shirt have something in common, unless we specify the respect in which Fido and your t-shirt are similar—that is, with respect to their color. But does this talk of respects not reintroduce the universal property color nominalists wanted to eliminate? Nominalists might demur at this point. They could propose to read "in respect of color" as qualifying the similarity relation adverbially: Fido and your t-shirt are similar-with-respect-to-color, and dissimilar-with-respect-to-size. On this reading, we should assume that there are two similarity relations in play here, one of which holds between Fido and your t-shirt, while the other doesn't. But this leads us directly to a second difficulty with this line of thinking. How should we conceive of similarity and resemblance themselves? Must these at least not be general relations that even nominalists have to accept in order to explain why Fido and your t-shirt resemble one another? (And the same would obviously hold for the more specific similarity-relations if these are needed.)

It is important to note that this latter problem is one that has been raised not only against nominalism, but also against trope theory; it's easy to see why. Trope theorists who hold that *all* properties are tropes have to address the question of how to do justice to the intuition that Fido and your t-shirt have something in common, because on trope theory there is literally no property they share. One answer that appeals to many trope theorists is to argue that Fido and your t-shirt have color tropes that resemble one another, and that this accounts for the intuition that there is something they both share. But here, again, the question of how to deal with the resemblance relation itself arises. Must this relation not be a general one that can be instantiated in many different cases and by many different objects?[4] Both nominalists and trope theorists, who try to explain the intuition that Fido and your t-shirt have something in common in terms of resemblance, have attempted to address this worry, for example by suggesting that resemblance is not a relation of the same kind as others. We cannot go into this debate in any detail here. But at least it should have become clear that nominalists still have considerable work to do in order to answer the third argument in favor of properties realism (and trope theorists as well, since the third argument does support realism about universal properties rather than particular ones).

Let us now turn to the fourth argument, the argument from realism about scientific practice. This argument relies on a specific understanding of natural laws which is not

4. This argument was developed by Russell (1912, chap. 9). For some answers from advocates of trope theory see Campbell (1990).

without alternatives. For instance, instead of regarding natural laws as connecting universals, some philosophers understand them as exceptionless regularities, which are described by universally quantified statements. Take the law "$v = vi + a \times t$" (velocity = initial velocity + acceleration multiplied by time). One could read this either as a statement about the relation between the universal properties of velocity and acceleration, or as stating that whenever an object is accelerated at a certain rate for a certain time, it has a velocity which is the original velocity plus the product of the rate of acceleration and time. The latter, universally quantified reading may have some drawbacks: for example, not all objects which fulfill the antecedent may also fulfill the consequent (e.g., if an object is abruptly stopped at the end of the period, reducing its velocity to 0). But in order to handle such cases, that involve for example outside interference or blocking, philosophers have developed strategies such as hedging the statement with *ceteris paribus* conditions. These strategies may hold some promise of success. However, how to understand laws of nature is not just a matter of getting the "technical details" of their proper formulation right. There is an underlying issue of whether one understands them as mere generalizations of the particular occurrences in the world, or whether one believes they have a special status that *underlies* and *explains* the generalities we can actually observe in the world. (On the first way of understanding them, the laws cannot be used to explain the generalities we observe; on the second, by contrast, they can be.) In the first case, the argument for universals that rests on realism about scientific practice is weak. In the second case, though, the argument has good prospects.

To recapitulate: in this section we have considered four of the most influential arguments for the existence of properties, and seen that while the first two are unpromising, the last two fare much better, even if they are not conclusive either. It seems however unrealistic to look for a definite knockdown argument for or against nominalism or realism. Rather, what this ongoing debate shows is that there are several (explanatory and metaphysical) pros and cons to weigh up when considering the question. On the one hand, positing the existence of properties incurs some costs, for we introduce a whole new class of entities in our ontology: they must earn their keep by playing an explanatory role in metaphysics. If they don't, the principle of ontological parsimony (don't multiply entities beyond necessity, as Ockham put it) forbids us to posit them. On the other hand, although this is a traditional and still mainstream way of thinking in metaphysics, we shouldn't assume that taking substances for granted and putting into question only other types of entity is our only theoretical option. There are also radically different alternatives, such as admitting only relations in one's ontology, or only properties, while taking substances to be derivative from more fundamental types of entity. For instance, advocates of ontic structural realism maintain that the relational structure of reality, as physics is "unravelling" it, is ontologically fundamental, and reject the idea that there are natures of objects that are independent of such relations. At one end of the wide spectrum of positions possible here, some of them maintain that this relational structure is all there is,[5] whereas at the other end of the spectrum others

5. See Ladyman and Ross (2007).

claim that substances exist, but that they have a relational nature.[6]

The fact that there are a number of metaphysical alternatives on the table does not mean, however, that the question has no possible resolution and that a positive stance cannot be taken. But whichever stance you end up with, you should be aware of the various pros and cons which it has. What we have tried to do in this section is to present the various alternatives and the main supporting lines of argument to give you a sense of the complexity of the debate and to motivate your own critical assessment of these arguments.

2.3 REDUCTIONISM AND FUNDAMENTALITY

In the last section, we have introduced the traditional debate concerning whether properties are to be admitted as entities in their own right in the ontology, alongside substances. In discussing this issue, we have appealed to considerations such as parsimony, which generally speaking encourages us to keep our ontology "lean," without introducing entities which are not needed. But keeping our ontology "lean" does not amount to eliminating all we can. In particular, there may be classes of entities that we are willing to allow in our ontology on account of the fact that they are (metaphysically) nothing "over and above" something else which we have reasons to accept in our ontology anyway. They come in as a "free lunch" to use D. Armstrong's expression.[7] In

6. For instance, Esfeld (2004).

7. Armstrong (1997, 12).

such cases it is sometimes said that a set of entities is "reducible to" others. To gain a better grasp of the distinction between elimination and reduction, consider the following two cases from the history of science. First, a case of elimination: in the eighteenth century, heat was thought to exist as "embodied" in a specific type of matter, caloric, which was then accepted as a *bona fide* existing entity. Later, it was discovered that the movement of molecules accounts for heat; hence there was no need to posit the existence of any additional matter that embodied it. So, caloric was eliminated from the class of things which physicists and philosophers considered to be real. Second, a case of reduction: for a long time, lightning was observed, but could not be scientifically explained. When it was discovered that lightning is (identical to) an electrical discharge in a certain meteorological setting—that is, when it turned out that the former is nothing "over and above" the latter—scientists did not, as a result, conclude that there exists no lightning, but rather that lightning is to be identified with, and thus be reduced to, electrical discharge.

Identification of one phenomenon with another is a particularly "neat" way to perform a reduction. Similarly, for instance, the deduction of one set of laws from another (together with the description of a specific setting and circumstances) is a particularly neat way to reduce the former set to the latter. But reductions are not always done this way, and the phenomena or the set of laws to be reduced cannot always be entirely "saved." In such cases, reduction involves some degree of elimination. Sometimes, for instance, what can be deduced is not exactly the original set of laws, but only one that is quite similar to it. Still, something which is still recognizably close to the original phenomenon or set of laws must be "saved"—else, there would be elimination rather than reduction of one phenomenon or set of laws to another.

For a period of time, the program of reducing certain classes of entities or phenomena to others was enthusiastically pursued by many philosophers, especially those of a logical positivist stripe. Advances in the natural sciences, which had allowed for the elimination of certain classes of entities (such as caloric) or the reduction of certain sets of laws to others (such as of the laws of thermodynamics to those of statistical mechanics), made it seem not an altogether implausible scenario that all kinds of entities could be reduced to a single set, e.g., those of microphysical entities, and all kinds of natural laws could be reduced to certain fundamental physical laws. Pursuing this project was one of the main aims of the Vienna Circle, which thought that all of the natural sciences could ultimately be derived from physics.[8] Achieving such a unity of the sciences was thought to be an attractive goal for reasons of ontological parsimony and explanatory economy. Furthermore, the idea was that we could reach genuine understanding of how reality "hangs together" overall only when such unity of the sciences would have been achieved (or at least, only when we would have some idea of what this unity would be like). This program has however been abandoned a while ago, and is nowadays considered unachievable. Not only have too many specific attempts at reduction of particular phenomena to others failed; it is also more and more widely thought that the different natural sciences have specific explanatory principles of their own, which cannot be deduced from simpler and more general ones. One

8. See, e.g., Carnap (1934).

underlying reason for this view is the realization that higher degrees of complexity can, at least in principle, introduce genuinely novel patterns of behavior that could neither be predicted from, nor explained *post factum* on the basis of, the principles in play in less complex settings. To take one well-known example (which we cannot however analyze here in detail): in quantum entanglement, the behavior of entangled entities cannot be deduced from the laws that govern the behavior of each entity considered singly.

The failure of the general reductionist project does not mean however that there aren't many interesting questions to be raised concerning how different phenomena in nature are related, and whether any of them are more basic than others. Answering the latter question in the affirmative does not necessarily imply that the entities which are less basic are redundant, or entirely reducible to the more basic ones. The question concerns whether one set of entities exists, or one set of facts holds, *in virtue* of (or *because of*) another set of entities or facts. For instance, when you look at a pointillist painting, and you see a figure of, say, a green tree, the shape that you see is there *in virtue of* and *because of* the arrangements of color dots on the canvas. Indeed, in the last decade, a growing number of metaphysicians have come to see as one of their main tasks to figure out not only what there is (i.e., which classes of things we should include in our ontology), but also how the things that exist are related in terms of fundamentality, and whether there is a hierarchy among what there is, such that some entities are more basic than others. The idea is that we cannot take a view on which theory of ours best describes the world unless we figure out the latter issues (e.g., Schaffer 2009, 372). Taking this additional task seriously is often viewed as a radical shift from the austere metaphysics of the logical positivists and the generation of analytical philosophers immediately following them, such as W.V.O. Quine. While Quine advised a very strict regimenting of one's ontology, famously expressing his preference for "desert landscapes" (1953a, 4), many modern metaphysicians are much more liberal in their ontologies, while stressing at the same time that figuring out what there is is only one of the tasks of metaphysics; deciding what is more fundamental is another equally (or even more) important task (See e.g. Schaffer 2009, 354). While we share the latter philosophers' sympathies for a more "liberal" ontology, we also believe that turning to such ontologies won't make many of the "old" issues about elimination or reduction simply "dissolve": instead, they will return in "new clothings" namely recast in terms of fundamentality. Therefore, abandoning the austere metaphysics of the logical positivists might not change as much as it may at first appear the set of philosophical problems we face- though it certainly involves a considerable revision of the substantive positions one takes on those problems.

2.4 DISPOSITIONAL PROPERTIES AND CATEGORICAL PROPERTIES

In section 2.2 we discussed the question of whether properties should be accepted as entities in our ontologies. Assuming this first question was answered in the affirmative, what *kinds* of properties should then be included? There is an enormous variety of properties objects have, and there are many different ways of classifying such properties. We can, for instance, distinguish between those properties objects possess just in virtue of the way the objects are themselves, without taking into account any relation they have to other objects, and those properties objects have only in virtue of standing in some relation to other objects; this gives us (roughly speaking) a distinction between *intrinsic* and *extrinsic* properties. For instance, being able to feel pain is an intrinsic property of yours *qua* human being, whereas being bigger than Fido is one of your extrinsic properties. We can also distinguish between *essential* and *accidental* properties for any given substance.[9] For instance, for Socrates, being human is an essential property that he could not lose while continuing to exist, while being married to Xanthippe is an accidental property of his. There is also a third distinction that we will discuss in this section, namely that between so-called *categorical* and *dispositional* properties (where the latter are also called powers, capacities, dispositions, and, more specifically, abilities).

In our everyday talk, we ascribe to objects both properties that characterize them as they are now, and properties that characterize what the objects might do, or how they would behave, under certain conditions. The latter type of property often exists in a "dormant" state here and now, and will (or can) exercise or manifest their powerfulness when appropriate conditions obtain. An object's size or shape, at least intuitively, fall under the first category (i.e., that of categorical properties), while its fragility or water-solubility fall under the second (i.e., that of dispositional properties). The glass is fragile here and now, but its fragility will manifest in its breaking, if the glass, say, is dropped from a certain height or on a certain type of surface. In our ordinary talk, we tacitly

---

9. See the discussion about the nature and essence of substances in chapter 3.

presuppose that categorical and dispositional properties are *on a par*, being both equally real properties of objects. A glass not only has a certain size, but also has a disposition to break when struck with appropriate force in appropriate conditions. After all, is this not the reason for which we handle fragile things with special care? Fragility thus seems to be a genuine property of the glass, with respect to which champagne flutes, china cups, and old parchments resemble each other. Yet many philosophers have held that dispositions are mysterious or "ethereal" properties (as Goodman [1983, 40] puts it), in a way that its size and shape are not. The reason for such skepticism about dispositions and powers is the following: shape and size are properties whose possession clearly determines how an object is *presently*. Things seem to be different with dispositions; for instance, a glass may be fragile without ever breaking. This suggests that when we ascribe a disposition or power to an object, we are not really talking about how the thing actually is—that is, about the properties it actually and presently possesses. What we are talking about, strictly speaking, is only its *possible* behavior and the properties it *could* acquire. Does this mean that powers are not really actual properties of objects at all? Some are inclined to think so.

Powers have—unsurprisingly—seemed even more "suspect" from an empiricist perspective. Categorical properties, such as size and spatial form, are directly perceptible and measurable. Powers by contrast are not directly perceptible: you do not see, by looking at a glass, that the glass is fragile. These empiricist worries played a crucial role in the widespread rejection of powers from the eighteenth century onward, which was due, particularly, to David Hume's highly influential critique of the realism about powers which had been prominent in the Aristotelian and Scholastic tradition. Hume tried to show that the concept of "power" did not meet the empiricist criteria of meaningfulness for concepts that he had developed, because it could not be traced back to any "original impression" (or "original experience"). Such impressions could only be had of "sensible qualities" which we could directly observe, such as color, shape, that "never point to any event that may follow from them."[10] This characterization of "sensible qualities" ruled out powers from the start, since, as we will see presently, "point[ing] to an event that might follow from them" is, on a widespread understanding of powers, their defining feature. Hume's worries about the inadmissibility of that which could not be directly observed reflect a more widespread concern which would have been shared by many philosophers back in his time—and, presumably, up to today—even when they would not have shared Hume's own specific version of empiricism. For did not the rise of modern science from the seventeenth century onward come with a commitment to experimental testing, and did this not, by itself, imply that positing entities whose existence could not be established by experiment and, thus, by observation, was problematic?[11]

In the next section we will argue that despite these worries, powers should be accepted as genuine and *bona fide* irreducible properties in the ontology. To do this, we

---

10. Hume, *An Enquiry Concerning Human Understanding*, 2000, 63.

11. This last worry lost its sting only by the developments in the theory of science in the second half of the twentieth century, which showed not only that all kinds of observation were, to some degree, dependent on background theory, but also that introducing theoretical entities was a fully licit tool in scientific theory-building.

have first to say something more specific about the distinction between powers and non-powers, that is, categorical properties.[12] What differentiates the former from the latter? As George Molnar has stressed, two features are essential to powers. First, their directedness:

> A power has directionality, in the sense that it must be a power *for, or to*, some outcome. It is this directedness that provides the prima facie distinction between powers (dispositions) and non-powers. (Molnar 2003, 57, emphasis added)

This outcome—that is, what the power is directed at—is usually called its manifestation or exercise; for example, fragility is directed towards breaking. The manifestation type defines[13] essentially the power type.[14] For example, solubility

---

12. Not all philosophers sympathetic to the idea that powers are *bona fide* properties believe that powers and categorical properties are two distinct classes of properties. Rather, some think that one and the same property is both dispositional and categorical. For instance, John Heil writes: "'A property's dispositionality and its qualitativity are, as Locke might have put it, the selfsame property *differently considered*"' (Heil 2003, 112, emphasis added). But even those philosophers have to say something about what distinguishes the dispositionality and the qualitativity of a property, and *this* question runs parallel to the question of how to distinguish between categorical properties and powers.

13. It is disputed whether other factors, such as the stimuli or manifestation-conditions, also essentially contribute to defining the power-type (e.g., Bird 2007, 7).

14. It is disputed whether each power (type) has *one* essential manifestation (type), or whether there can be several manifestations (types) for one power (type). This is the dispute over whether there are only single-track, or also multi-track powers. E.g., arguably, the negative electric charge of an electron can be manifested both in repelling another electron or in attracting a positively charged particle. We cannot go further into this debate here.

is essentially the capacity of something to dissolve in water. In contrast to powers, categorical properties, such as size or shape, are not essentially directed at a certain manifestation. This gives us a rough-and-ready distinction between powers and categorical properties. The actual occurrence of a power's manifestation is not however essential to the possession of a power by an object; or in other words, as Molnar puts it, "Powers are ontologically independent from their manifestations. They can exist even when they are not being exercised" (2003, 57). Thus, a glass may possess the property of being fragile, even though it never actually breaks. This ontological independence from their manifestations is the second key feature of powers, according to Molnar.

Can we sharpen this first distinction between dispositional and categorical properties into something more precise? A natural way to proceed might be to appeal to language, and use the existing distinction between dispositional and nondispositional *predicates* (or *concepts*) that we already have available in our ways of talking in order to draw the distinction between categorical and dispositional properties. There are however at least two major difficulties with this approach. First, as we saw in section 1.2 of chapter 1, the relation between properties and predicates is not straightforward—we cannot simply assume that to any meaningful predicate there corresponds a property. (Recall the famous counterexample provided by Russell.) So, how can we be confident that the distinction between two kinds of properties neatly maps the distinction between two types of predicates? Second, it is not clear that we have a good understanding of the distinction between dispositional and nondispositional predicates that is independent from our understanding of the distinction between two kinds of properties. To begin with, dispositional predicates come in many different forms. Some are formed by attaching suffixes like –ile, or –ble to verb-stems (e.g., being fragile, or breakable), or by adding "disposed to" in front of verbs (e.g., being disposed to break); but sometimes we create completely new words (e.g., being elastic or negatively charged). Again, some dispositional predicates are directly connected to conditional statements, such that their ascription allows us to infer these latter statements. Take the case of water-solubility, for example: when an object is water-soluble, we can infer that under right conditions, it will dissolve when coming into the right kind of contact with water. Other dispositional properties, by contrast, don't work that way. For instance, "x is an unstable explosive" does not tell us anything about the conditions under which x will explode. This large variety we find in the form and behavior of dispositional predicates can easily make us feel suspicious about whether there is a single class of properties that corresponds to them, that is, the class of dispositional properties or powers. Even if we just focus on dispositional predicates whose ascription is necessarily related to conditional statements, the distinction between categorical and dispositional properties is not easily drawn. Take a disposition like water-solubility, where the effect, in appropriate conditions, *has* to obtain if the conditions for manifestation are present, so that we can infer, from possession of the disposition, that the corresponding conditional holds. This seems to provide the basis for a criterion for distinguishing dispositions from categorical properties, namely, that when possessing the former and certain conditions obtain, the object will necessarily behave in a certain way; while this would not hold for categorical properties (e.g., Bird 2007). Let us call this a modal criterion, as it stresses that powers or dispositions are governed by a certain modality, that is, conditional necessity (see also section 3.5 of chapter 3). There are, however, categorical properties too that appear to fulfill the modal criterion. Take a paradigmatic categorical property such as the size of an object. A ball with 10 cm diameter will necessarily fall through a round hole of 10 cm diameter if we drop it into the center of this hole (*ceteris paribus*, and excluding outside interventions). So, there seems to be a conditional expressing the behavior of the ball that we can infer from the ascription to the ball of the categorical property of being of a certain size. Of course, one might say that the respective connections between the ascriptions of dispositional and categorical properties and the relevant conditionals are importantly different. For water-solubility, the conditional is, in a sense, defining the kind of property it is; while the same doesn't seem true for categorical properties. But it has proved very difficult to draw this distinction in clear and noncircular terms that did not covertly presuppose the linguistic distinction between different kinds of predicates or concepts we have talked about. So, perhaps the distinction between dispositional and categorical properties is not as clear as it at first appears, in the sense that even putatively categorical properties might meet the given criteria for being "dispositional," so that all properties will turn out to be dispositional ones. This is an option many philosophers have come to take seriously in the last fifteen years, and in section 2.6. we will also consider the theoretical option that at the fundamental level of reality there are only dispositional properties.

For the time being, let us proceed with the rough distinction between powers and categorical properties that we have elaborated so far: powers, by contrast to categorical properties, are essentially directed at certain manifestations, while their possession is independent from their exercise. In contrast to the case of categorical properties, the connection to these manifestations is "defining" for the kind of property a power is.

2.5 ARE POWERS GENUINE AND IRREDUCIBLE PROPERTIES?

With this distinction at hand, let us return to our question of whether powers should be admitted in our ontology as *bona fide* properties in their own right. Here is again the worry that realism about powers faces, as expressed by Nelson Goodman:

> The dispositions or capacities of a thing—its flexibility, inflammability, its solubility—are no less important to us than its overt behaviour, but they strike us by comparison as rather ethereal. And so we are moved to inquire whether we can bring them down to earth; whether, that is, we can explain disposition-terms without any reference to occult powers. (Goodman 1983, 40)

How can disposition-terms be "brought down to earth"? One strategy is that of providing a reductive analysis of the statements which use disposition- and power-terms, such that in the analysis all talk of dispositions or powers is eliminated (recall the discussion of reduction and elimination in section 2.3). For, after all, it is the use of these terms which has initially suggested to us that such properties as powers exist. If it could be shown that these statements can be understood without supposing that there are dispositional properties in addition to categorical properties, our chief reason for admitting powers into our ontology would vanish. Skeptics about powers have indeed tried to provide such analyses. One of the most influential analyses of disposition-ascriptions was the conditional analysis proposed by Gilbert Ryle:

> To possess a dispositional property is not to be in a particular state, or undergo a particular change; it is to be bound or liable to be in a particular state, or to undergo a particular change, when a particular condition is realized. (Ryle 1990, 43)

More schematically, we can put the point as follows. On the conditional analysis,

> Something is disposed at t to give response r to stimulus s iff: if x were to undergo stimulus s at time t, then x would give response r.

The conditional analysis of disposition-ascriptions is *prima facie* attractive, because it exploits the connection between many disposition-ascriptions and conditionals that we have already noted in section 2.4 of this chapter. But it is nowadays mostly accepted that the conditional analysis is unsuccessful. A particularly important role in refuting this analysis has been played by cases of so-called finks and masks. Fink and masking cases have shown that satisfying the right-hand side of the bi-conditional in the analysis is neither necessary nor sufficient for the object in question to possess the relevant disposition.

In fink cases (which C. B. Martin [1994] was the first to draw attention to), if the appropriate stimulus for the exercise of a power were to occur, it would impact on the possession of the power itself. Take the property of "being (electronically) live." That, for example, a metal wire is live, would, according to the conditional analysis, be equivalent to "if the wire were to be touched by a conductor, the electric current would flow from the wire to the conductor." Imagine now that a wire is dead, but is connected to an electro-fink, that reliably registers when the wire is about to be touched by a conductor; if it is, the fink will instantaneously make the wire live for the duration of the contact. In this case, the counterfactual conditional that is proposed as an analysis for "the wire is live" is satisfied: if the wire were to be touched by a conductor, the electronic current would flow (because it would be made live then). Nonetheless, at the present moment, the wire is dead. This shows us that fulfillment of the conditional is not sufficient for having the disposition in question. Similarly, it is not hard to imagine "reverse" cases, where a reverse-fink makes a live wire dead when a contact is about to occur. Such "reverse-fink" cases show that fulfillment of the conditional is not necessary, either, for having the disposition in question. Both fink and reverse-fink cases share a general structure, namely that either the stimulus itself, or something connected to the stimulus, would make the object either lose or acquire the power in question *just when* the stimulus was about to occur. This change of the relevant powers of the object, if the stimulus was about to occur, is essential to the set-up of these cases. This feature explains why the conditional analysis has fundamental difficulties with such cases, because the analysis does not admit the existence of powers as genuine properties. (Recall the eliminativist program driving this analysis.) And if you don't regard powers as genuine properties, it is unsurprising that you will find it difficult to account for cases where these powers seem to be acquired or lost just as other properties are.

So-called masking cases differ from fink cases insofar as they do not involve a change in the possession of the relevant power. Instead, in such cases, the power's full manifestation is, or would be, blocked by other causal factors. For instance, the poison's power to kill an organism when ingested may be blocked by the antidote's power if the latter is ingested in time (Molnar 2003, 93). In such cases the conditional, which is meant to be equivalent to the disposition-ascription—which conditional, for the poison's power to kill, would be something like "if x were ingested by y at time t, x would kill y"—is false, but nonetheless the object (i.e., the poisonous substance) possesses the power in question (i.e., the power to kill an organism when ingested).

On account of these widely acknowledged difficulties with the conditional analysis of power-ascriptions many philosophers have moved to a causal analysis of power-ascriptions. Schematically, this analysis goes as follows:

> Something x is disposed at time t to give response r to stimulus s iff: x has some property P that would cause x to give response r if x were to undergo stimulus s at time t.

Obviously, if this is to be a reductive analysis of power-ascriptions, P cannot itself be a power, but has to be a categorical property, which is sometimes called the categorical base of the power or disposition. Does this new analysis avoid the problems which the conditional analysis faces, or does it run into new ones? There remain grounds for pessimism. First, fink cases seem to remain in the picture, even if they become slightly more complicated. Consider again our reverse-fink case, where the wire is live, but would be made dead by the fink if a conductor were about to touch the wire. The fink would now have to do this, presumably, by making the wire lose its categorical property P. But if it does so, the conditional which is meant to analyze the possession of the disposition "being live" is still false, even though the wire is presently live. The same applies *mutatis mutandis* to masking cases.

In addition, the causal analysis encounters a further problem, namely the problem of deviant causal chains. For, even when the stimulus and a categorical property P which the object possesses cause the object to give response *r*, they may do so in the "wrong" way for the response to be a manifestation of the power in question. The following case illustrates this point: assume that some rubber which is not water-soluble has the categorical property of being ball-shaped. Merlin, a magician who hates ball-shaped objects when wet, decides to destroy that rubber ball if it ever comes into contact with water; he would do so by making it water-soluble by magic if the ball was about to touch water. Thus, with regard to this particular rubber, it is true that it has a categorical property—namely, its being ball-shaped—which would cause it to dissolve were it to be put into water (because it is its shape that would motivate Merlin to cast his spell and make the rubber water-soluble). Nonetheless, at present, when there is no water around, the rubber is not (yet) water-soluble.

Different amendments have been proposed to save the causal analysis from these and other problems. (The best-known one is Lewis's [1997] proposal, which tried to prevent fink cases, by postulating that the property P had to be retained for some time after the stimulus's occurrence.) These amendments however have only given rise to yet more complicated counterexamples. We cannot go through all the further ramifications of this debate here. Of course, the problems that have arisen for the analyses of power-ascriptions proposed so far do not establish that no reductive analysis of these ascriptions is possible. Perhaps some analysis immune to counterexamples will be found at some point. But the odds are against this outcome, and by and large metaphysicians nowadays have come to believe that such a reductive analysis is not feasible, because it would either be ultimately circular, or involve such overly complicated conditionals that it would have little chance of telling us what dispositional statements really had in common.

This has led to a general shift in metaphysics, in the last thirty years or so, toward accepting powers as *bona fide* properties in the ontology. The failure of the reductive analyses of power-ascription has been an important factor in motivating this change of view, but not the only one. Another important factor has been scientific realism, and the recognition that many sciences include powers (such as electric charge, mass, spin, etc.) in their account of natural phenomena, and even include them among the fundamental properties of nature for which no further analysis can be provided. Furthermore, there is ever increasing interest in metaphysics in trying to account for natural laws, and the necessity which is associated with them, in terms of powers. The thought is the following: if dispositions characterize how an object must behave under certain conditions, they account for a certain kind of necessity that we see in play in the natural world, that is, physical necessity: as long as the powers of two electrons are what they are, these electrons *must*, *ceteris paribus*, repel one another (see also 3.5). Physical necessity, thus accounted for in terms of the powers objects in the world have, might then be used to explain the status of natural laws. This is a further reason why powers are thought to do important metaphysical and explanatory work in the ontology, thus earning their keep as *bona fide* entities.

Adopting a realist stance concerning powers has widespread ramifications in many areas of metaphysics and philosophy in general. (One particularly important area where realism about powers is likely to make a crucial difference is the debate about causation, to which we will turn in chapter 4.) Our next task is to examine the question of whether, in light of the considerable force of the arguments in support of power realism and the difficulties in distinguishing powers from categorical properties, we might have reasons to hold that that *all* properties are powers, at least on the fundamental level of physical reality. To this issue we turn now.

2.6 AN ONTOLOGY OF PURE POWERS?

Are powers all we need in our ontology? According to a view that is currently enjoying considerable popularity in metaphysics the answer is positive, at least with respect to the fundamental level of reality. On this view everything else, including substances, is derived from powers. Further, a version of the theory that is gaining traction is that all properties are "pure" powers. What does "pure" mean in this context? The relevant distinction is between powers that are necessarily "anchored" to a categorical base – or have themselves a categorical aspect - and powers that are not; the latter ones are called "pure." Take for instance the water-solubility of a sugar cube, which, it seems, necessarily depends on the sugar having some internal structure such that it can be dissolved.[15] By contrast, consider the electric charge of an electron, which does not seem to have any categorical aspect or to be anchored in any further categorical property of the electron. (It cannot be anchored in any further categorical property, because the electron is defined in terms of its constitutive powers, such as charge, mass, and spin.) Could all fundamental properties in physics be "pure" powers? Contemporary physics gives us reasons to take this option very seriously. In addition, the view that some powers are "anchored" in non-power properties is not without difficulties of its own.[16] In the following, we therefore want to explore the prospects of the pure powers view as an account of what properties there are at the most basic level of nature, and to see how it fares with regard to the main difficulties that have been raised against it in the literature.

The best-known criticism of the view that the fundamental building elements of the world include only pure powers is the so-called *always packing, never traveling* argument, according to which in a world of pure powers change would merely correspond to the transition from a potential state to another potential state, without there ever being any change in the *actual* properties or states. Following C. B. Martin (1993), David Armstrong presents this argument as follows: in an ontology which only admits pure powers as genuine properties,

---

15. Without such a structure, we could not even imagine that it "dissolves."

16. See, e.g., Bird 2007, chapters 1 and 4.

particulars would seem to be always re-packing their bags as they change their properties, yet never taking a journey from potency to act. (Armstrong 1997, 80)

Armstrong's argument raises the problem that on the pure powers view nothing would ever "really happen," and things would ever remain "in mere potency." Why? Because the activation of a power would be a mere instantaneous leap from that power in potentiality—that is, its being present, but not yet manifested—to its manifestation, which would be just another power in potentiality. This means that powers, on this view, would never be truly manifested or exerted: they necessarily remain "in potentiality" (before being replaced by another power). But a theory that does not allow supposedly activated powers to exert their power would be quite odd—and yet this seems to be the position of those who claim that the manifestation of a power in potentiality is just another power in potentiality.[17] The problem seems to lie in this particular assumption about powers and their manifestations however, rather than in the pure powers view itself. This becomes clear when we look at the following reply which has been offered in response to Armstrong's argument by Stephen Mumford and Rani Anjum:

> On reflection, the idea of causation as a passing around of powers, especially for a pandispositionalist, starts to look extremely attractive . . . Armstrong retorts that such causation, for pandispositionalism, consists in the mere passing around of powers. In the present case, that would mean that the heat of the fire, which consisted in it having the power to warm some

17. For instance, Mumford and Anjum write: "The manifestation of a power will . . . be itself a further power or cluster of powers" (2011, 5).

other object, has been passed on to you. But that sounds quite
right. (2011, 5–6)

By buying into a "passing around" account of causation,
Mumford and Anjum seem to allow no place for the manifestation of a power which goes beyond its transfer or exchange
with another power merely "in potentiality." How are we even
to make sense of this "passing around" without any further
account of how it happens? What is the mechanism of the
transfer of powers such as, for example, the power to warm
another object? Is the same token power instance somehow
transferred from the fire to you, does the fire lose its power,
or is its power duplicated? (Without a better account of the
individuation criteria for token powers which are meant to
be in play here, there is not even a beginning of an answer to
these questions in sight.) Furthermore, even if one accepted
the thought that powers are "passed around", what reason is
there for thinking that this provides an exhaustive account
of the changes happening in that situation? How would the
"passing around" account apply to other cases, for example,
in the case of a vase that breaks? Which power(s) would be
passed around in such a case?[18]

An alternative response to Armstrong's argument has
been offered by Marmodoro (2014 and 2017a), who argues
that a power and its manifestation are not distinct items;
rather, the manifested power is the very same power as the
one in potentiality, but in a state of activity. This view draws
on Aristotle's account of powers, and is radically different
from accounts like Mumford's and Anjum's which hold that
the manifestation of a power is a *new* power that comes

18. See Marmodoro (2017a).

about.[19] On the alternative view, by contrast, this is not the case: it is not the case that a new property comes about in place of the original power when the original power manifests. Rather, the manifestation is a different state *of the very same* power.

This difference in the conception of the powers' manifestation can also be put in a different way. On Mumford's and Anjum's (and others') conception, powers are construed as relational properties: they are taken to be essentially *related* to further powers in potentiality and to their manifestations.[20] A neo-Aristotelian power ontology such as that of Marmodoro, by contrast, is *not relational*. For a power in potentiality is the same power as when being manifested; so being manifested does not relate a power to a further power in potentiality. If this is correct, then a neo-Aristotelian view that takes all properties to be powers has the resources to avoid Armstrong's *always packing, never traveling* objection.

We have seen that Armstrong's argument loses its bite once we reject the view that when a power is manifested it is simply transferred or replaced by another power in potentiality. John Heil raises another objection to an ontology of pure powers, however, with an argument which is similar, yet not identical, to Armstrong's. Heil's argument focuses on the hypothesis that in a world of pure powers, the object on which a power exerts its causal efficacy is nothing but a bundle of powers in potentiality. Heil writes:

> Suppose *A*s are nothing more than powers to produce *B*s, *B*s are nothing more than powers to produce *C*s, *C*s are nothing

19. See Marmodoro (2017b).

20. See, e.g., Mumford and Anjum (2011).

more than powers to produce *D*s ... and so on for every concrete spatio-temporal thing. How is this supposed to work? Imagine a row of dominos arranged so that, when the first domino topples, it topples the second, which topples the third, and so on. Now imagine that *all there is* to the first domino is a power to topple the second domino, and *all there is* to the second domino is a power to be toppled and a power to topple the third domino, and so on. If all there is to a domino is a power to topple or be toppled by an adjacent domino, nothing happens: no domino topples because there is nothing—no thing—to topple. (Heil 2003, 98)

The hypothesis that in a world of pure powers the object on which a power exerts its causal efficacy is nothing but a bundle of powers in potentiality is however implausible, because powers such as that of the domino piece to topple another piece presuppose the complexity of the object that bears them, as well as other properties of that object (such as its size, mass, shape, hardness, etc.). Many of the powers of a domino are constantly activated, manifesting themselves in the presence of other powers of the domino, even when the domino's power to topple is not manifested. Ultimately, contrary to Heil's assumption, a domino that can be toppled *exists*, and this domino *is something more* than the power (in potentiality) to topple (or to be toppled by) something else.[21]

Neither Armstrong's nor Heil's argument thus provide a decisive reason to believe that all properties at the fundamental level of reality could not be pure powers. You might still think that, even at the microphysical level, further

21. Marmodoro (2017a).

properties are needed which are not purely dispositional, such as spatial properties. But then, on the one hand, spatial properties are not intrinsic properties of objects, so at least the theoretical option remains open that all intrinsic properties on the microphysical level are pure powers. This is a good thing, given that modern physics takes this option very seriously. On the other hand, according to one influential view, spatial properties are relational properties, a view famously held by Gottfried Wilhelm Leibniz—and it is doubtful whether relational properties exist in their own right as well. This is the issue to which we must turn in the last section of this chapter.

2.7 RELATIONS *VERSUS* MONADIC PROPERTIES

Until now, we have debated the issue of realism or anti-realism only with respect to monadic properties, that is, properties that individual objects have of their own and even when considered singly.[22] Let us now turn to relations, such as "being bigger than" "being at a certain distance from," which, it seems, connect different objects. Partly, the issues raised by relations are the same as those raised by properties (in particular, they largely overlap with respect to the realism versus nominalism debate), but there are some additional complications for relations that we will consider in this section. In particular, the question arises whether we need relational properties in addition to

---

22. This section draws partly on Marmodoro and Yates (eds.), (2016), "Introduction."

monadic properties, or whether the former can be reduced to the latter.

One motivation for thinking that we should do without relations and relational states (unless these can be reduced to monadic properties and non-relational states) is a problem, which Kit Fine (2000) has pointed out for the case of nonsymmetric relations. A relation R is nonsymmetric if aRb does not entail bRa; for instance, in the case where Abelard loves Heloise, Heloise may not conversely love Abelard. According to a proposal put forward by Russell, since there are two possible directions for such relations (from Abelard to Heloise and from Heloise to Abelard), nonsymmetrical relations "hold together" their relata with an inbuilt directedness. On this view, the two possible directions (from Abelard to Heloise and from Heloise to Abelard) correspond to two different relational states.[23] However, as Fine notes, this implies that to love and to be loved are necessarily distinct relations. Intuitively however, it would seem that "Abelard loves Heloise" and "Heloise is loved by Abelard" describe one and the same relational state, and that there is only one single relation between the two. To avoid this problem, some philosophers deny that there are relational states or relations altogether, even though they still countenance relational truths. For them, those truths are made true by the instantiations of monadic properties. For instance, the sentence "Socrates is taller than Plato" is true, on their view, because of the instantiation by Socrates and Plato

23. See Russell (1903).

of monadic properties such as "being 185 cm tall" and "being 180 cm tall."[24]

The view that all relations can be reduced in this way to the possession of monadic properties by individual objects might appear somewhat counterintuitive, but it has a long tradition. For Plato, Aristotle, and the majority of medieval philosophers, there are no irreducible relational properties. Aristotle considers relations such as "to be the slave of" as reducible to monadic properties that Sicinnius and Themistocles possess. It is crucial to note that those properties are not simply "to be a slave" and "to be a master," but instead "to be the slave *of*" and "to be the master *of*," respectively. Sicinnius's property "to be slave of" somehow points to Themistocles, and the corresponding property of Themistocles "to be master of" points to Sicinnius. Thus, what might seem as the instantiation of a single relational property between Themistocles *and* Sicinnius and possessed by both, for Aristotle, is instead the instantiation by them of two distinct monadic properties, each one in a sense directed towards the other: "to be the slave of" and "to be the master of." Despite the fact that neither Plato nor Aristotle describe explicitly in their works such a reductive view of relations, their texts support attributing this position to them. A first reason for this interpretation is that for the ancient thinkers, properties are instantiated by individual subjects. In particular, for Aristotle this is true because individual substances are the primary beings in the ontology, and properties depend on them (as we have seen in chapter 1). Individual subjects like Themistocles and Sicinnius have ontological

---

24. However, there is no agreement on the claim that all relational truths can indeed be explained in this way.

"boundaries" that demarcate each individual subject's being, according to the Aristotelian criteria of substantiality as expressed in the *Metaphysics* VIII 3. As a consequence, in Aristotle's ontology there can be no relational properties, since they would weaken the ontological supremacy and the boundaries of each substance. Relational properties would belong equally to all the n relata of an n-adic relation, as if they were divided and distributed between all subjects involved (Sicinnius and Themistocles, in our example). A second reason for the absence of relations in ancient ontologies is that for the thinkers of that period, it is not possible that two separate individuals taken together form a single object, say a dual subject composed, for instance, by Themistocles and Sicinnius. (Aristotle explicitly rejects that substances can compose into substances.) But this is exactly the type of subject that would be needed to bear a polyadic relational property, in order to keep attributes within the ontological boundaries of substances. Third, for ancient thinkers, properties are features that qualify individuals in one way or another. For instance, the nature of the property Red that inheres in an apple is what explains (metaphysically) the color of this particular apple. Asymmetric polyadic relations like "to be the slave of" would have no role of this sort to play, were they included in the ontology. How could a single polyadic relational property explain, for example, Themistocles being a master and Sicinnius being a slave? Even if we assumed the existence of a subject composed by the two individuals bearing this relational property (which, we have seen, ancient thinkers would not accept), how could a single property of this kind explain all the different characterizations of that emergent subject, relative to the multiple subjects that compose it? For it should explain different things about Themistocles and about Sicinnius, namely that one is the master and the other is his slave, and it is unclear how it can do this.

However, the idea that polyadic relations can be reduced to instances of monadic properties reciprocally directed ceased to be widely held at the beginning of the twentieth century, mainly due the work of Bertrand Russell (1903, §§212–14). Russell claimed that Aristotle's theory cannot eliminate relations, because the alleged monadic properties that the theory relies on have a relational aspect. The reason, for Russell, is the following: as noted, for Aristotle, Themistocles doesn't possess the property "to be master of" *simpliciter*, but rather he is "master of" relative to Sicinnius. In the same way, Sicinnius is not a slave *simpliciter*, but relative to Themistocles. But what does having a property relatively to something else mean?

> In the first way of considering the matter, we have "L is (greater than M)," the words in brackets being considered as an adjective of L. But when we examine this adjective it is at once evident that it is complex: it consists, at least, of the parts *greater* and M, and both these parts are essential. . . . The supposed adjective of L involves some reference to M; but what can be meant by a reference the theory leaves unintelligible. An adjective involving a reference to M is plainly an adjective which is relative to M, and this is merely a cumbrous way of describing a relation. (Russell 1903, 214)

Russell's point is that while we can talk about Themistocles's property using a complex one-place predicate "is the master of Sicinnius," this does not entail that the property is really monadic. For Russell, to be the master of Sicinnius entails standing in a relation with Sicinnius, and hence what appears *prima facie* to be a monadic property ("being the master of Sicinnius") is in fact a relation in disguise. When we describe it by a one-place predicate, as Russell puts it, this is "merely a cumbrous way of describing a relation." So, for Russell, the attempt to do away the prima facie relation "is the master of" in terms of the instantiation of monadic properties is doomed to failure. The majority of contemporary metaphysicians accept this objection, and hold that if we accept properties as entities on their own in our ontology, then we also have to accept relations. Nonetheless, those who are skeptical about the irreducibility of relations to monadic properties don't yet consider their cause as lost. There are at least two different approaches they can take in responding. They might argue case by case that specific putative relational truths are true due to the instantiation of monadic properties; or they can provide a general argument against the idea of irreducible relational properties. As we have seen, ancient and medieval philosophers favored the latter strategy, while contemporary metaphysicians, who are skeptical about the existence of relations, are inclined to adopt the former strategy. Given its necessarily piecemeal approach, it would be premature to predict that this former strategy must fail—but given the difficulty raised for the reductionist view by Russell, we do think it has little chance to account for all cases of relational truths we should accept.

2.8 CONCLUSIONS

In this chapter we have examined properties and relations. In particular, we reviewed some arguments in favor of and against their inclusion in the ontology as *bona fide* entities, which led us more general issues concerning reduction and eliminativism in metaphysics. Assuming that properties are *bona fide* entities in our ontologies, we then discussed some of the most recent developments in the metaphysics of powers. Since the latter are paradigmatically modal properties, this discussion naturally leads us to our next topics: essentialism and modality.

*

MODALITY AND ESSENCE

3.1 INTRODUCTION

Metaphysics is concerned with the question of what kinds of things there are and what they are like; but it is also concerned with the question of how things *could be*, or *must be* – that is, with possibility and necessity. When in everyday talk we say that something must be such-and-such, or could be such-and-such, many different senses of necessity (and, correspondingly, of possibility) may be in play. To get a flavor of the variety of different senses, consider the following three statements which all concern (im)possibility:[1]

a) Nothing can travel faster than light. (This is a law of nature.)
b) You couldn't have been born to different parents. (A person born to different parents would not be the same person.)
c) You cannot be asleep and not asleep at the same time. (This would be a logical contradiction.)

---

1. For further discussion of these (and more) kinds of modality see Kment (2017).

These three examples describe different kinds of impossibility, or necessity. The first example concerns a *physical* impossibility relative to the laws of nature of our world, whereas the second concerns *metaphysical* impossibility, which is not based on laws of nature but on the essential properties of the object involved (in this case, you). The third case illustrates *logical* impossibility, which follows from the meaning of the terms and connectives used in the sentence.

Logical necessity is a kind of necessity accepted by nearly all philosophers. Several other forms of necessity have often been explained in some way or another in terms of logical necessity, for instance by taking the modal statement in question to include a covert "relativization" to a certain group of statements which are taken as fixed. "It is physically necessary that p" could, for instance, be read as "Given the laws of nature, it is necessary that p." The truth of the statement would then depend on whether the laws of nature entail p or not, and entailment is directly tied to logical necessity. By contrast, statements of the second type, b), are not easily reformulated as statements of the form: "Given that q, p is necessary." What b) says is that some properties are essential to you, where essential properties are meant to be properties without which you could not be the individual object you are.

Making sense of metaphysical possibility and necessity presents a major challenge to metaphysicians. In this chapter, we will investigate whether they can meet this challenge by appeal to essential properties of objects. We will therefore discuss the nature of essential properties and the doctrine of essentialism in some detail. We will first present Aristotle's highly influential version of essentialism (in section 3.2). Afterwards, we will move on to the developments of essentialism in the twentieth century, and examine how this theory was criticized within the tradition of logical positivism which dominated early analytic philosophy, when necessity and possibility were generally viewed to be properties of statement or propositions, not of objects or ways of being (section 3.3). A key role in this development was played by Quine's rejection of essentialism, which became the orthodoxy in the middle of last century's positivist climate. The situation changed considerably with Saul Kripke's groundbreaking development of a new semantics for modal statements, in terms of possible worlds, which made it possible to more clearly express the difference between *de dicto* and *de re* necessity statements (section 3.4). Following the developments of this new semantics, the 1970s saw a new surge in neo-essentialist views (e.g., Kripke 1980; Plantinga 1979; Fine 1994; Mackie 2006). We will conclude this chapter with a discussion of how realism about Aristotelian powers provides us with alternative ways to understand modalities other than by appeal to possible worlds (section 3.5).

3.2 ARISTOTLE'S ESSENTIALISM

As we have seen in chapter 1, it is intuitively very plausible to distinguish between the properties an object possesses only accidentally, and those it possesses necessarily, such that it could not continue to exist without retaining these properties. Poodle Fido could continue to exist even if he ceased being a pet dog. (We can easily imagine that he runs away one day and becomes a stray dog roaming the streets.) But being a dog is not a property Fido could likewise lose: he could not have been a flower, a house, a cat, or any other kind of thing, and still have been Fido, namely, the particular being he is. When we introduced the notion of essential properties of an object in chapter 1, our description might have suggested that they are simply properties that an object necessarily possesses when it exists. Indeed, in contemporary metaphysics this has, for a long time, been the standard view (until Kit Fine's influential critique). Stated more formally, the idea is that

F is an essential property of $x =_{df}$ if x exists, x necessarily possesses F.

Traditionally, the essence of a thing, or its essential form, was thought to consist not of *all* the necessary properties of this thing however, but only of those properties that made it the kind of thing it is, and determined its nature. Not all properties an object necessarily possesses, whenever it exists, belong to this more limited set of its essential ones. Take Fido. As long as Fido exists, he will necessarily have the property of either being identical to the number 9 or not being identical to 9. But this property does not make Fido the kind of thing he is. Rather, it is a property any object has, *whatever* its nature may be.[2] Also, existence has long been held to a property of things, and if this is true, existence is obviously a property an object must possess as long as it exists; but existence has not traditionally been considered an essential property of objects (except, arguably, of God).

In Aristotle too we find a narrower understanding of essence, which can already be seen from some of the host of loosely related locutions that Aristotle uses in discussing

---

2. For other cases of this kind, and further criticism of the necessary possession account of essential properties, see Fine (1994).

essences. One preferred locution of his is *to ti ên einai* (the "what it was to be"), which is an abbreviated way of saying "that which it was for an instance of kind *K* to be an instance of kind *K*"; for example, "that which it was (all along) for a human being to be a human being." On Aristotle's view, what it is to be a human being is just what it always has been and always will be, namely to be rational. This feature is meant to be captured in his essence-specifying account of human beings (see, e.g., *Analytica Posteriora* 75a42–b2; *Metaphysics* 103b1–2, 1041a25–32). This essence, for Aristotle, has both an "exclusive" and an explanatory function: he assumes, first, that there is some feature F that all *and only* humans have in common and, second, that F explains the other features we find across the range of humans.

It is therefore crucial for Aristotle that the distinction between properties an object has only accidentally (such that it can lose them without ceasing to exist) and its essential properties is not exclusive, since his ontology includes also an important class of necessary, but non-essential properties. In particular, beyond the purely logical features that are not specific to any kind of being or any substance and are therefore ruled out from being essential properties by "exclusivity" considerations (such as the property of either being identical or not identical with the number 9), Aristotle recognizes a category of properties which he calls *idia*.[3] These are properties that "flow from" the essence of a kind, such that they are necessary to objects of this kind, without being essential to them. For instance, if "being rational" is essential to human beings, then it will follow that every human being

---

3. See for example *Categories* 3a21, 4a10; *Top.* 102a18–30, 134a5–135b6.

is necessarily "capable of grammar". For while "being capable of grammar" is not the same property as "being rational", that you have this former property follows, for Aristotle, from your being rational. Since Aristotle also thinks that only rational beings are capable of grammar, the property of "being capable of grammar" cannot be ruled out by the exclusivity test, either, because "being capable of grammar" will be an exclusive property of human beings if "being rational" is. But the latter property is more basic, in the sense that our rationality explains our capacity for grammar, even though, necessarily, something is rational if and only if it is also capable of grammar. Because it is explanatorily prior, "being rational" has a better claim to being (part of) the essence of human beings than "being capable of grammar" does. The criterion of explanatory priority gives the essence a unifying role with regard to the other properties the object has, since one and the same essential property will explain many different features the object has necessarily or accidentally. Consequently, Aristotle's essentialism is considerably more fine-grained than a view that simply identifies essential properties with necessary ones. According to Aristotle's essentialism:

F is an essential property of $x =_{df}$ (i) if x loses F, then x ceases to exist; and (ii) F is (objectively)[4] an explanatorily basic feature of x, since F accounts for other necessary properties of x.

---

4. This presupposes some account of the criteria according to which an explanation is objectively good, and of the criteria according to which a feature is explanatorily more basic than another, that make comparative basicness not fully context-dependent. Otherwise, either of two interconnected features might count as more basic, depending on context.

3.3 AGAINST ESSENTIALISM AND NON-LOGICAL NECESSITY: QUINE'S CRITIQUE OF *de re* NECESSITY

The assumption that some properties are possessed essentially, or even merely necessarily, by objects, in the way described in the last section, underlies the traditional distinction between *de re* and *de dicto* modality. When the statement "*x* is necessarily F" is read as expressing a necessity *de re*, it can be read as attributing to X the necessary possession of F (i.e., saying *of x* that it is necessarily such that it has F).[5]

(*De re* reading) X is (necessarily-F).

By contrast, when it expresses a necessity *de dicto*, it can be understood as stating that the embedded statement "*x* is F" is necessarily true. Thus, on the *de dicto* reading, the statement "*x* is F" lies within the scope of "necessarily," and "necessarily" is naturally read as a sentence operator attached to this embedded sentence, that is, as

(*De dicto* reading) Necessarily (x is F).

On the *de re* reading, by contrast, when "necessarily being F" (as one complex property) is predicated of *x*, the "necessarily" cannot be understood as a sentence-operator, but rather as an adverb generating a new complex predicate from

---

5. It is plausible to view this as ascribing a new property to X, namely the property of "having F necessarily," see Plantinga (1999, 141).

a simpler one (namely the predicate "necessarily-being-x" from the simpler one of "being-x").

That there are necessities and possibilities *de dicto* is uncontroversial; at the very least, it is widely accepted that when we attach "necessarily" to a logical or conceptual truth, we get a *de dicto* necessity. "Necessarily, if it rains, it rains" is true because "If it rains, it rains" is a logical truth; and "Necessarily, bachelors are unmarried" is true because "Bachelors are unmarried" is a conceptual truth. What about *de re* necessities or possibilities? The acceptance of *de re* necessities has a venerable tradition and is part and parcel of essentialism (since essential properties are a subclass of necessary properties of objects). However, it was much criticized in the first half of the twentieth century, along with essentialism, before it enjoyed a major revival in the 1960s and 1970s. The objections that were raised against *de re* modalities have to be taken seriously, because they show that accepting modalities of this kind is far from trivial, and that we must examine carefully whether we have a good enough grasp of them. One main concern, which Quine put forcefully forward, stems from the fact that once we understand

(1) x is necessarily F.

as attributing to (object) x the necessary possession of F, this would entail, by Leibniz's law, that whenever we substitute a co-referring singular term for "x", the resulting statement should still be true. For, thus read, (1) attributes *to x* a certain property (the property of having F necessarily), and *if x* has that property at all, it must have it no matter how we refer to or describe x. (Just as, when we ascribe to Octavian the property of being Caesar's nephew, then if Octavian is identical to the first Roman emperor, also the first Roman emperor must have the property of being Caesar's nephew.) Now take

(2)   9 is necessarily greater than 7.[6]

If we suppose that we can ascribe necessary possession of a property to an object at all, (2) seems a pretty good candidate for such an ascription: 9, it seems, could not be the number it is without being greater than 7; if a number were smaller than 7, then it would have to be another number than 9. (Of course, we might still *call* a number that is smaller than 7 "9," because we have decided to change our number-words and have renamed, for example, 3 as "9." But this would not change the fact that the number that we are currently calling "9," as we use the term now, cannot but be greater than 7.) However, we also have

(3)   9 = the number of planets.

And by Leibniz's law

(4)   For all x, y: $x = y$ if and only if for all P (Px iff Py)[7]

we thereby get

(5)   The number of planets is necessarily greater than 7.

6. See Quine (1953c, 143).

7. In plain words: for all objects x and y: x is identical to y if and only if all things attributable to/true of x are also attributable to/true of y, and *vice versa*.

But (5) is false; the number of planets could easily have been different, and may even be different at some future point (e.g., when one planet is destroyed by a meteor). Since (3) and (4) are unexceptionable, it seems we can only avoid the apparently unacceptable (5) by either abandoning (2) altogether or by giving it a *de dicto* reading, that is, as

(2*)   It is necessarily true that 9 is greater than 7.

For from (2*) we do *not* get (5), because here "necessarily," understood as a sentence operator, introduces an intensional context. To such contexts, Leibniz's law does not apply and in them substitution of co-referring terms *salva veritate* is not possible.

However, when the objection is presented in this way, defenders of *de re* modality can easily complain they are being misinterpreted.[8] For, as they can object, when we take (5) to be clearly false, we do so only because we give it a *de dicto* reading, understanding it as

(5*)   It is necessarily true that the number of planets is greater than 7.

Adopting this reading is unfair to the defender of *de re* necessities, because she wanted to read (2) as expressing a *de re* necessity, rather than a *de dicto* one, and therefore can only be committed to (5) when that statement is understood as expressing a *de re* necessity, too, and is not committed to (5) when it is given the *de dicto* reading (5*). If we took her to be committed to (5*) as well, we would saddle her with an

8. Cf. Plantinga 1999, 144f.

additional commitment to specific cross-modality inference rules allowing derivations of *de dicto* necessities from *de re* necessities. Such additional commitments are neither necessarily included in the view the defender of *de re* necessity subscribes to, nor are they independently plausible. So, what the defender of *de re* modalities is committed to, is the only the inference from (2) to

> (5**) The (actual) number of planets (i.e., the number which is *de facto* the number of planets) is such that it is necessarily greater than 7.

Assuming we can make sense of (5**), it is not clearly false. Rather, it sounds just the right thing to say. For the phrase "the (actual) number of planets" picks out the number 9, and, if (2) is true, then 9 is indeed such that it is necessarily greater than 7. So, once the "necessarily" in (2) and (5) is given a uniform reading (i.e., in terms of *de re* necessity), it seems that if (2) is true, (5) will be true as well.

So far, so good.[9] But while this move suffices to avoid the unwanted result that the defender of *de re* is committed to (5*), it presupposes that we can distinguish between two different kinds of properties of objects (in our case, the number 9), namely those properties objects have essentially or necessarily, and those they have only contingently. Only by doing so, we can say that what "the number of planets" really picks out is the number 9, and can then use the necessary or essential properties of this number to account for the truth of (5). If, by contrast, all the properties of 9 were on a par (if, e.g., its being the number of planets was a property it held just like

---

9. Quine, admits the possibility of such a move, in (1960, 199).

all its mathematical relational properties to other numbers), then we wouldn't be able to explain why (5) is true while the sentence

(6)   9 is necessarily such that it is the number of planets.

is false. (6) is surely false, whether understood *de dicto* or *de re*. (Neither is it necessary that there are exactly 9 planets, nor would the number 9 cease to be the number it is if one planet was destroyed.) So the crucial question becomes whether we can draw a distinction between necessary and contingent properties of individual objects. Quine thought that we could not; or, to be more precise, he thought that any such distinction would have to rely on having already subsumed the object in question under a certain kind or type of thing. Objects could have properties necessarily only *qua x* or *considered as an x*. For instance, I *qua* human being necessarily have the property of being rational (assuming that by definition all human beings are necessarily rational); but this is true because the property is included in the definition of being human, such that my having this property logically follows from my being human. Without specifying an individual object as falling under a certain type (relative to which type we can distinguish between properties that are conceptually included in the definition of this type and properties which aren't), the distinction between necessary and contingent properties does not make sense, Quine argues, and therefore cannot be applied to objects considered as such and not *qua* something. For, otherwise one would easily end up with contradictory ascriptions of necessary properties. As Quine puts it in a well-known passage:

Mathematicians may conceivably be said to be necessarily rational and not necessarily two-legged; and cyclists necessarily two-legged and not necessarily rational. But what of an individual who counts among his eccentricities both mathematics and cycling? Is this concrete individual necessarily rational and contingently two-legged or vice versa? Just insofar as we are talking referentially about the object, with no special bias towards background mathematicians as against cyclists or vice versa, there is no semblance of sense in rating some of his attributes as necessary and others as contingent. Some of his attributes count as important and others as unimportant; some as enduring and others as fleeting; but none as necessary or contingent. (1960, 119)

As Quine acknowledges, essentialists who accept a distinction between essential and contingent properties of an object will deny the last point. But the distinction they want to draw, Quine goes on to say, "however venerable . . . is surely indefensible."[10] Ultimately Quine's rejection of *de re* modality thus derives from his rejection of individual essences. Objects have properties necessarily only *qua* objects of certain kinds, or *qua* falling under certain descriptions. Since no kind or description of an object is privileged, in the sense that it would specify what the object *really* is (and not just happens to be contingently), any description true of the object will yield statements about properties the object has necessarily *qua* member of this kind or bearer of this description. The necessity in play here is clearly language- and description-dependent and comes down to a kind of *de dicto* necessity. But if *this* is Quine's challenge to the defender of *de re* necessities, essentialists will be optimistic that they can

10. Quine (1960, 119f.).

meet it. After all, it is precisely their contention that there are individual essences and the properties included in them are, with regard to that object, "privileged" over other properties the object also happens to have.

The defender of *de re* modalities can also draw on further general considerations to reject Quine's argument. For Quine's response would no longer work if, in referring to an object, we were necessarily referring to it *qua* object of some particular kind or other. If that was the case, then the properties this object would have *qua* object of this kind, would indeed be privileged *vis-à-vis* its other properties, and would be such that the object could not lose them without ceasing to be that particular object. Some influential considerations concerning reference and the possibility of reidentifying objects that have been put forward by Peter Strawson (1959) suggest that this picture might be indeed the right one. When I pick out a certain object, Strawson argues, I cannot just refer to it under no description whatsoever, even when I say for instance "that object over there." Why not? In order to refer to the object at all, I must be able to individuate it, and to distinguish it from other objects. If by "that object over there" I mean to refer to the desk rather than the chair, I must be able to distinguish the object I am referring to from the chair. Furthermore, I must, in principle, be capable of reidentifying over time the object I am referring to now (i.e., I must be able to determine whether a later referential act refers to the same object, or a distinct one). Criteria for reidentification for particular objects are provided by sortal concepts; for instance, "dog" or "chair." If this reasoning is correct, we can never refer to (particular) objects under no description whatsoever; we can only refer to them as falling under certain sortal concepts (namely, concepts which specify what "kind of thing" we are talking about, and provide criteria for individuation for it). This line of thought will easily lead to sortal essentialism (at least for substances), namely the view according to which the properties specified in the sortal concepts are essential properties of the substances which fall under them. For, when the criteria for reidentification of an object provided for by e.g. the sortal "human being" include that the object in question is rational, then I cannot continue to exist as the same human being if I lose my rationality. Furthermore, being a human being is not just one description among many that must be true of me as long as I exist: it is the one that provides the criteria for individuating me as a particular object. For the individuation criteria for me *cannot* be provided by different sortals at once,[11] since the criteria provided by such different sortals could conflict, in which case I would not have any determinate individuation criteria at all. If successful reference requires sortals, these sortals thus provide a range of properties an object must have as long as it exists and that determine what kind of being it is.[12]

Two methodological points about this reply to Quine merit emphasis. First, this reply does not hinge on the claim that objects can have properties independently of falling under any type of object. On the contrary, it shows that objects may have to fall under certain types and thus may necessarily have those properties included in the definition of these types. It therefore meets Quine's criticism on

11. We leave here aside the case where one sortal is the more specific form of a more general one, such as "human being" and "animal."

12. See, e.g., Wiggins (2001), who offers a very sophisticated account of sortals.

its own grounds. Second, the reply harnesses considerations from philosophy of language (concerning the conditions for meaningful referential acts) in order to draw substantial metaphysical conclusions; that is, to support a version of essentialism. This might come as a surprise to the reader who thinks that metaphysics is concerned with what there is or must be, while how we think and talk about the world is a completely different matter. But it would be wrong to presuppose that the latter has nothing interesting to tell us about the former. If we find out that we can only make sense of certain key features of our core lingustic practices by assuming that the world is in a certain way, then this gives us a good reason to assume that the world is indeed in this way, if we are confident enough that these features and activities do make sense. And, taking the case of referential acts, it is natural to assume that, in everyday life, we usually refer successfully to objects in the external world (leaving aside possible skepticism about the external world). In this case, philosophy of language thus provides indirect support for interesting metaphysical conclusions.

3.4 THE REVIVAL OF *de re* NECESSITY AND ESSENTIALISM

The general change in attitude towards essentialism that occurred during the 1960s and 1970s was mainly due to two groundbreaking contributions by Saul Kripke: his development of a possible world semantics for modal statements, and his influential argument for the possibility of *a posteriori* necessary truths. We will introduce these two ideas in turn.

3.4.1 Possible worlds

Kripke's possible world semantics was the first easily applicable and powerful formal semantics for modal statements, and soon came to be the default view in the philosophical debate. This semantics develops from the following intuitive idea: when we say that an actual object x could have been different, we can naturally interpret this as tantamount to saying that there is a possible counterfactual (i.e., nonactual) situation *in which x is different.* That your dog Fido could have had brown fur (instead of the white fur he has) can naturally be read as "there is a possible (nonactual) situation in which Fido has a brown fur." Possible worlds can be understood (as a first approximation, at least) as aggregates of such counterfactual situations. If we take the talk of "world" seriously here, we will also assume that they have a certain completeness, such that, at least, for each *object x* that exists in this world and all properties P, it is uniquely determined *whether x* has P or not.[13]

Not all worlds are possible. For example, a world in which Fido is totally white and not totally white at the same time is not possible, because a situation of this kind is excluded by logic. Let us leave such impossible worlds aside, though, and consider only the worlds that are possible. Kripke suggested that we can then understand necessity and possibility in

---

13. Usually, possible worlds are understood as even more inclusive than that, cf. Lowe (2002, 82): "A possible situation is 'maximal' just in case it satisfies the following condition: for any proposition p, either it is the case that p is true in the situation in question, or else it is the case that p is not true (and hence that not-p is true) in the situation in question." Similarly, Menzel characterizes possible worlds as "single, maximally inclusive, all-encompassing situation[s]" (Menzel 2016).

terms of quantification over these possible worlds. To say that it is possible that p (e.g. that Fido has brown fur), is to make the existentially quantified statement that there is *at least one* possible world in which p is true (Fido has brown fur). Formally:

$\Diamond$ p iff there is a possible world W such that W $\parallel$ p.
("W $\parallel$ p" is the formal expression for "in world W, p is true.)

To say that it is necessary that p, is to make the universally quantified statement that in *all* possible worlds p is true.[14] Formally:

$\square$ p iff for all possible worlds W, W $\parallel$ p.[15]

This move of accounting for the truth conditions of modal statements in terms of quantification over possible worlds has an enormous advantage: it allows us to bring the well-developed ordinary non-modal logic of quantifiers into our analysis of modal statements. For, on the suggested analysis, the logical form of "It is possible that Fido has brown fur" is the same as that of "There is a dog that has four legs" (since it is irrelevant to the logical form that we quantify over very

14. Sometimes this analysis is qualified by the further requirement that we are only looking at possible worlds that are "accessible" from the world in which the modal statement is evaluated for truth or falsity. I.e., "Fido necessarily has brown fur" would count as true in the actual world even if there was a possible world in which Fido did not have brown fur, as long as that world was not accessible from the actual one.

15. Note that at this point, we are not talking about *de re* necessity yet. The necessity statements we are evaluating are statements were the necessity attaches to the substatement p, and the same goes for the possibility statements.

different things in both cases: over possible worlds in the one case, and over dogs in the other). We can therefore use the comparatively well-understood formal apparatus of quantification for our semantics of modal claims in order to assess the soundness of arguments in which such claims appear as premises and conclusions. This is, undeniably, a major gain.[16]

The framework of possible worlds has been applied more widely than to the analysis of statements concerning possibility and necessity; in particular, it has been used to provide a semantics for counterfactuals. As David Lewis has argued,[17] such a semantics can be provided once we introduce the notion of *comparative overall similarity of possible worlds*. Take a counterfactual conditional such as "If it had rained today, the street would have been wet tonight." When is such a statement true? Since the conditional is a counterfactual one, this cannot depend on whether the antecedent and consequent are true as things actually are. (For a material conditional, this would be different: a material conditional is automatically true if the antecedent is false. But certainly this is not true for counterfactual conditionals as we normally understand them, since there clearly are false conditionals of this sort. For example, "If it had rained today, the street would have been dry immediately afterwards" is false under most circumstances.) Rather, Lewis suggested, we have to look at the non-actual situations in which the antecedent is true (i.e., in which it did rain today), and examine whether the consequent is true in them or not. We

16. More on this in e.g. Lowe (2002, 121).

17. For more detail see Lewis (1973).

do not however look at all the possible situations in which the antecedent is true; doing so would fail to determine a unique truth value for our counterfactual, since in some of these situations the street is wet tonight and in others dry because someone has dried up the street during the day. We only look at those situations that most closely resemble the actual course of events, that is, we make the least possible departure from reality and keep the background and surrounding facts fixed, as far as possible. So, ideally, in evaluating our conditional "If it had rained today, the street would have been wet tonight," we look at situations that are *just like what actually happened* apart from the rain and its consequences. If in such situations the consequent holds true (i.e., if the street is wet in the evening in this scenario), the counterfactual as a whole is true; if not (e.g., because the street has a fail-proof drainage system), it is false.

Lewis tried to cash out this intuitive idea of "the least possible departure from reality" in terms of the notion of similarity between possible worlds. Different worlds, he argued, resembled one another more or less closely with respect to the particular facts and the laws that held in them. Lewis thought that on the basis of these two aspects we could impose a similarity-ordering on possible worlds, such that we could compare whether worlds A and B resembled each other more closely *overall* than, e.g., worlds A and C. Having introduced this notion of closeness (in resemblance), we can then sharpen the intuitive idea of "least departure from reality" in the following way:

Let "A $\square\rightarrow$ C" stand for the counterfactual "If A had been the case, then C would have been the case." Let an "A-world" be a world in which A is true; analogously for "C-world." Then we get the following truth conditions for counterfactuals:

"A □→ C" is true if either

(1)   there are no possible A-worlds (i.e., it is impossible that A);
      or
(2)   some A-world which is also a C-world is closer to the actual world (actuality) than any A- world which is not also a C-world.[18]

(1) is a situation in which the counterfactual is said to be "vacuously true"; while (2) is meant to render more precise the earlier idea that "a counterfactual is true, if it takes less of a departure from actuality to make the antecedent true along with the consequent than to make the antecedent true without the consequent."[19] Since (2) is thus the crucial alternative for the analysis, let us briefly consider two different situations to see how it works.

In the scenario depicted by Figure 3.1, the possible world(s) in which it was raining which is (are) closest to the actual world is (are) clearly somewhere on the line between D and E. All possible worlds on this line are also ones in which the street was wet, because the line between D and E falls within the grey square. So in this scenario, the counterfactual statement "If it had rained, the street would have been wet" comes out true.

In the scenario depicted by Figure 3.2, by contrast, while the nearest possible world(s) where it was raining lies (lie) somewhere in the middle of line B–C, this world (or these

---

18. This formulation may appear overcomplicated; why don't we look at just the one closest possible world in which the antecedent is true? Because we can only do so if there is a unique closest possible world of this kind, and this is an assumption that Lewis didn't want to make.

19. Menzies (2014).

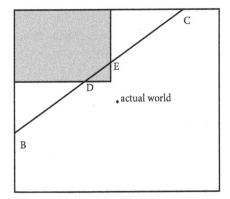

Line B-C divides worlds where it is raining (left top) from worlds where it isn't (right bottom)

The grey square contains those worlds where the street is wet.

FIGURE 3.1 Counterfactual Rain 1.

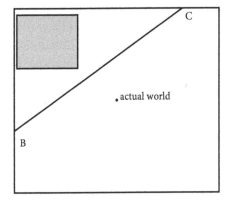

Line B-C divides worlds where it is raining (left top) from worlds where it isn't (right bottom)

The grey square contains those worlds where the street is wet.

FIGURE 3.2 Counterfactual Rain 2.

worlds) is (are) not a world (worlds) in which the street was wet, because it does (they do) not fall within the grey square. So, in this scenario, the counterfactual "If it had rained, the street would have been wet" comes out false.

Let us bring to a close this excursion into the semantics of counterfactuals, for the moment. (We will return to it in chapter 4, in discussing Lewis's analysis of causal statements.)

What is important for our purposes here is that the framework of possible worlds has proved fruitful, as far as its use as a formal model is concerned. This is neither to say that it is without its pitfalls, nor that the semantics which is based on it perfectly fits all our intuitive assessments of modal statements. In part, these pitfalls and worries concern the more technical details—for instance, whether it even makes sense to think of possible worlds that are "complete" in the way described earlier, or how we are to determine whether the object we are talking about in one world can be the same as the object we are talking about in another world. (For instance, is the Fido who is white in the actual world the same entity as the one who is brown in another world—or is the other-world Fido merely a counterpart to the actual Fido? This is the so-called problem of transworld identity.) But there are also more fundamental concerns regarding the ontological status of the possible worlds that make up this framework. Are they to be taken to be real entities (and if so, are they only, and do they only involve, abstract entities; or particular entities too)? Or is the "possible world" talk merely a useful formal device, or a useful "as if" way of talking, which does not commit us to believing there really are any such things (contrary to what robust modal realists such as Lewis [1986a] suppose)? Despite the popularity of modal realism among metaphysicians who follow Lewis, major difficulties lie in going the first way. Indeed, Kripke himself mocked this approach for taking "the metaphor of possible worlds much too seriously . . . It is as if a 'possible world' were like a foreign country, or distant planet way out there" (1999, 78). At the very least, considerations of ontological parsimony speak in favour of taking possible worlds talk to be merely a useful, merely formal device or "as if" talk which does not bring extra ontological commitments with it. In addition, semantics of modal statements based on possible worlds does not capture all of our ordinary thinking about modality. It allows us to draw certain distinctions that would be hard (or even impossible) to state in non-formal language, while neglecting other distinctions, that can no longer be drawn in this framework. As long as we regard the framework of possible worlds as a useful tool, this is unobjectionable—no tool is perfect. But it would be highly problematic to assume that this framework introduces an ontology of possible worlds that really exist and are necessary to justify our everyday talk about what is possible or necessary.

After this brief overview of possible worlds approaches to modality and counterfactuals, one might ask: how does this help us with regard to *de re* modalities? Is not the semantics offered here a semantics for necessity when "necessarily" is understood as an operator attached to whole sentences? Have we not seen that for *de re* modality we cannot understand "necessarily" in that way? The reply is that once the framework of possible worlds is in place, it does allow us to finesse and make more formally rigorous the notion of *de re* modality, which shows that this notion is clearly to be distinguished from *de dicto* modality. Take the statement

(7)   Aristotle is necessarily human.

and read it as a statement about necessity *de re*. What will the truth conditions for (7) be within a possible worlds semantics? They will *not* be:

(8)   In every metaposhysibcale possible world Aristotle is human.

(8) would be the analysis for (7) only if (7) was understood as a *de dicto* necessity statement. (For obviously, if p is necessary *de dicto*, p is true in all possible worlds.) Instead, (7) will be true iff

(9)   In every possible world in which Aristotle exists, Aristotle is human.

(9) captures nicely the idea that being human is a necessary property of Aristotle (on the *de re* reading of (7)) such that he could not exist without having this property. (Note that the latter is crucially different from necessarily existing and necessarily having this property.) So the possible worlds framework gives us, as an added benefit, a formally more rigorous semantics for *de re* modality statements as well. But this is just for starters; together with a further crucial notion of Kripke's, it does something else as well. To see this, we must turn to the second major factor in the revival of *de re* modalities in the 1970s, namely Kripke's argument for *a posteriori* necessary truths.

3.4.2 *A posteriori* necessity

Two distinctions have played a central role in the modern debate about necessary truths and how we can cognize them: the distinction between necessary and contingent, and the distinction between *a priori* and *a posteriori*. The distinction between *a priori* and *a posteriori*, which was most famously put to use by Immanuel Kant in the *Critique of Pure*

Reason, is an epistemological one that concerns the dependence of (instances of) knowledge on perceptual experience. *A priori* knowledge does not depend on and is not derived from any specific experience or sensory input, while *a posteriori* knowledge does depend and is derived from such input.[20] Thus, to take a paradigmatic case of *a priori* knowledge, knowledge of the mathematical truth that 2 plus 2 equals 4, when it is obtained by means of ordinary mathematical derivation,[21] is neither based on, nor requires, empirical or experiential input about how groups of pairs combine. (You didn't, and couldn't in principle, acquire this knowledge by checking empirically whether for all given pairs of objects, adding two such pairs gave you always a group of four objects.) Knowledge of the fact that it is raining, by contrast, as a paradigmatic case of *a posteriori* knowledge, can only be acquired by looking outside, or checking the weather in some other way that involves experience. These two cases already suggest that the distinction between *a priori* and *a posteriori*, on the one hand, and the distinction between necessary and contingent, on the other, are closely aligned. For knowledge

20. Perhaps we all need *some* experience or sensory input in order to have any knowledge or cognition at all; without such experience our cognitive faculties might remain dormant, as it were. But at least *a priori* knowledge does not require our having experiences with any *specific* content which is related to what we have *a priori* knowledge of, while *a posteriori* knowledge does require that.

21. This qualification is important, because you *could* even acquire knowledge of logical truths in a way essentially relying on experience. Instead of doing the logical derivations yourself, you could, e.g., learn this truth from someone whom you have sufficiently good reason to consider as a fully reliable authority in these matters. Since the latter way of acquiring knowledge would rely on experience—concerning the other's reliability—the knowledge gained in this way would be *a posteriori* knowledge.

of the mathematical truth that 2 plus 2 equals 4, which is *a priori*, is also knowledge of a necessary truth, while *a posteriori* knowledge of the fact that it rains is knowledge of a contingent fact. To express such alignment, we could say that for every necessary truth, it will at least be possible to have *a priori* knowledge of it, while this will not be possible for a contingent truth. However, as Kripke pointed out, we cannot expect complete alignment here: the distinction necessary/contingent is a metaphysical distinction, while the distinction *a priori/a posteriori* is an epistemological one, and we cannot just assume that these two different distinctions coincide. In addition, Kripke claimed, if essentialism is true, there will be necessary truths that can only be known *a posteriori*. Assume, for instance, that among the essential properties of Kripke's lecture lectern is that it is made out of a particular kind of material, and assume further that, *de facto*, this material is wood.[22] Then, in all the worlds in which this lectern exists it will be made out of wood, and the statement

> (10) Necessarily, if Kripke's lectern exists at all, it is made out of wood.

will be true (assuming Kripke's semantics for modal statements). But we do not know, and could not have known *a priori* which stuff the lectern was made of. We had to look and see which stuff that was. What we did know *a priori*, arguably, was that if it was made out of stuff P, then it was necessarily made out of stuff P. But in order to draw the inference that the lectern was necessarily made out of wood, empirical input was indispensable.

22. See Kripke (1999, 81).

The possibility of *a posteriori* necessary truths is crucial for those philosophers who espouse an essentialism that goes significantly beyond the sortal essentialism we have discussed at the end of section 3.3. For sortal essentialists, the essence of an individual object is not something you discover, by means of empirical inquiry, after you already know which object you are talking about. For according to Strawson's argument that we set out in section 3.3 you will need to know what sort of thing you are talking about in order to refer to this object at all. But if you believe that there is more to an individual object's essence than what is specified by the sortal it falls under (but also, e.g., which material it consists of)—and many philosophers have followed Kripke in making this assumption—, then statements about the object's essential properties will be necessary, but they will not be knowable *a priori*.

A posteriori necessary truths are of interest not only in relation to the essences of individual objects, but also in relation to to the essences of kinds. Especially natural kinds—such as basic physical kinds or elements, or biological kinds such as species—are often held to have an essence. Take a statement like

(11)   Water is necessarily H_2O.

This has been considered by many philosophers to be true. However, it does not follow from the meaning of "water" that water is H_2O—much empirical research was needed to establish that. So if (11) is true, it is at best an *a posteriori* necessary truth. But is (11) merely a statement of physical necessity—that is, that according to the natural laws which actually obtain, water is H_2O—or does (11) express the nature of water and count as case of a metaphysical necessity? Kripke developed a highly influential account of how it could do the latter, which was based on his notion of rigid designators.

A rigid designator is "a term which designates the same object in all possible worlds" where this object exists (Kripke 1999, 77). Many designators we use are non-rigid, in particular all those definite descriptions that might have applied to another object than the one they do actually apply to. Take the description "the first European to sail around the Cape of Good Hope." As things actually turned out, the first European to sail round the Cape of Good Hope was Bartolomeo Diaz. But there are many counterfactual situations in which the first European to accomplish this feat was somebody else, for example, Christopher Columbus. While in the actual world "the first European to sail around the Cape of Good Hope" designates Bartolomeo Diaz, in these other possible worlds it designates some other person, such as Christopher Columbus. Since it designates different objects in different possible worlds, it is a non-rigid designator. By contrast, as Kripke claimed, some classes of designators function as rigid designators; for instance, proper names.[23] But, as Kripke (in his 1980) and, in a similar vein, Hilary Putnam (1975, ch. 12) have contended, natural kind terms also work in this way. This claim is at first sight surprising, when we take a natural kind such as water. Do we not identify water by the observable properties we normally associate with it, such as being a liquid, being transparent, quenching thirst, or dissolving salt? Could not

---

23. This proposal has not however been uncontroversial, for it threatens to imply that proper names lack descriptive content.

these properties, which are, in our actual world, possessed by (sufficiently large aggregations of) H_2O (molecules), be possessed by some other stuff (e.g., sufficiently large aggregations of XYZ molecules) in some other possible world? Is that not something we can fairly easily imagine? Would water not be XYZ (rather than H_2O) in that other possible world? Both Kripke and Putnam would answer in the negative. Of course, they would agree that in this other world people might *call* XYZ "water" (if, say, the history of their acquisition of the concept "water" was sufficiently similar to ours). But the word "water," as *we* use it, could not be applied to XYZ under these changed circumstances. Why? Because we do not use "water" as an abbreviation for a definite description or a cluster of such descriptions, and water does not mean "the stuff that is liquid, transparent, or quenches thirst." We only use that description and these properties of water to identify water. Water is the stuff that, *in the actual world*, has these properties, and we use "water" to refer to *that* stuff, whatever it may be and even in situations where it does not actually play these roles or have the properties which we have originally used to pick it out. For, we use the designator "water" rigidly, in Kripke's terms. This stuff, which in the actual world plays this role, is H_2O, not XYZ. So even in a possible world in which XYZ had all the properties and functional roles of H_2O, water would still be H_2O and not XYZ. In consequence, (11) comes out as involving metaphysical necessity rather than just physical necessity. For in any possible scenario in which water exists, it will be identical to H_2O, even if the laws of nature were different—which precisely fits the characterization for *de re* necessity we gave at the end of section 3.4.1 (when we adapt it to kinds rather than individual objects).

Kripke's insistence that water will continue to be H_2O even in the described alternative scenarios shows that he doesn't take the essence of water to consist in its perceptible properties. Rather, for him, it is the underlying microstructure that has the better claim to constituting water's essence and which explains, in the actual world, the perceptible properties water has. Whether this is true is, unsurprisingly, hotly debated, and intuitions on whether something that shares none of the perceptible macro-qualities that water has could still count as water diverge widely. In consequence, not only Kripke's notion of rigid designators, but also its particular application to natural kinds, have been hotly contested. It is nonetheless true that for the mainstream of analytic philosophers these notions have played a considerable role in reinstating *de re* necessities as a "respectable" part of the metaphysical discourse and in "rehabilitating" essences.

The conception of essence, which was rehabilitated in the wake of Kripke's work, looks, at first, quite different from the Aristotelian conception of essence, since Kripke's account of essences refers to microphysical structures that would have been completely inaccessible to Aristotle. But there is a stronger underlying continuity here, at least as far as the objects of the natural sciences are concerned. Both Aristotle and Kripke turned to what they considered the best scientific account of their time to identify and explain the essences of natural objects. Where the sciences in question differ (quite dramatically) between Aristotle's time and ours, their answers will necessarily widely differ. For instance, Aristotle would think that water is essentially transparent, while Kripke would think that there are possible worlds where H_2O is not transparent, because the wavelength of light is different from that in our world. But Aristotle's and

Kripke's methodology—their relying on the best scientific account of their days—was not that dissimilar, after all.

3.5 POWERS AND MODALITY

In chapter 2, we discussed at some length the recent revival of interest in powers and dispositions as *bona fide* properties. It is therefore natural to ask whether the "reappearance" of powers on the metaphysical scene should influence our understanding of modality and of metaphysical necessity too. Do powers provide us with an alternative way to think about modality, an alternative to the framework of possible worlds? Since having a power means that you can do certain things (in a specific sense of "can"), there is likely to be *some* connection between powers and possibility. But which connection precisely? This is the question that will concern us in the final section of this chapter. To address this question, it will be helpful to start by articulating why an account of modality based on powers seems attractive. One, and possibly the main motivation is that it would provide a way of "anchoring" modalities in the way actually existing ordinary objects are.[24] Such an "anchor" is missing in accounts such as Lewis's that try to explain possibility merely in terms of possible worlds within which potentialities or possibilities are absent.

Let us expand on this point, focusing on metaphysical possibility. Take a statement like "It is (metaphysically) possible that a spaceship travels faster than light." (That a

24. For further discussion and references to other work on this topic, see, e.g., Vetter (2015, 11).

spaceship does so is incompatible with the laws of nature, as they hold; but presumably nothing in the nature of traveling through space or the nature of spaceships rules out that they could achieve a greater speed than the speed of light.) On Lewis's account this statement is true because there is some relevant possible world in which spaceships do achieve this greater speed. On this picture, the metaphysical possibility is indeed "anchored" in the properties of *some* object(s)—but these objects are not actual objects, but "otherwordly" ones that only exist in nonactual worlds. For it is the spaceships *in these other possible worlds* that make the statement "It is (metaphysically) possible that a spaceship travels faster than light" true, and *not* spaceships or other objects in *our* world. This seems problematic, on different counts. Not only does it remain unclear why we should assume that such "otherwordly" spaceships exist at all. It is also far from obvious why their supposed existence and properties should tell us anything about what is true *in our world*.[25] Our statement that it was metaphysically possible that spaceships travel faster than light was meant to be about our (actual) world. But on Lewis's account, it is not a statement about actual spaceships or about spaceships that will actually exist, or, for that matter, about any actual or future thing at all. So, you might wonder, has Lewis's analysis not simply "changed the subject" of the original statement?[26] The answer is: Yes, Lewis has "changed the subject". For Lewis shares the Humean

---

25. The issue here is a slightly different one from the question of whether we should think of individual objects as existing "in parallel" in many different possible worlds, or as only having counterparts in other possible worlds. For our statement is not about any particular spaceship.

26. For a more detailed discussion of this objection see Jacobs (2010, 230f.).

misgivings about powers that we considered in section 2.4, and believes that there are no such properties in the world. When we look at situations within one possible world taken by itself, for Lewis, these are "modally empty;" it is only by looking at the relations between possible worlds or by quantifying over possible worlds that we arrive at modal statements.

Having "stripped" the actual world of modality and powers, Lewis has to appeal to other, non-actual, worlds in order to provide an account of modality. (But note that these other worlds, too, are themselves bereft of modality.) Modality becomes not an "intra-world", but a "trans-world" feature, as it were. However, as we saw in chapter 2, Hume's misgivings about powers aren't compelling; powers are genuine properties. Accepting them in our ontology gives us a way of finding modality *within* the actual world, thus making the framework of possible worlds potentially re-dundant for explaining modality. Talking about possible worlds might still be a useful *façon de parler*, but we need not be committed to modal realism (i.e., the view that pos-sible worlds really exist) in order to make sense of mo-dality. In addition, if we succeed in showing that what makes modal statements true are the powers actual things have, this will be a way to "anchor" possibility in how actual things actually are—and if we can do that, it will be fairly obvious why making a statement about possibility tells us something about our (actual) world. (Once you have pos-sibility, you can easily account for necessity too, using the interdefinability of both notions: that p is possible iff it is not necessary that not-p.)

So, trying to explain metaphysical possibility in terms of powers is certainly an attractive project; but how can it be done? Several different ways have been proposed, which, while differing in details and complexity, share the general idea that statements of the form "p is possible" can be explained in terms of some actual object's having a power or disposition such that its manifestation would make it true, or bring it about, that p.[27] To get a better idea how this might be fleshed out, let us look in more detail at one such proposal, which has recently been made by Barbara Vetter. (Note that Vetter uses the term "potentiality" for power or disposition.) Her proposal is as follows:

> POSSIBILITY: It is possible that p $=_{df}$ something has an iterated potentiality for it to be the case that p.[28]

Why does the notion of an "iterated" potentiality come in here? Plausibly not everything that is possible is so because of how actual things (already) are. Sometimes it is only possible that something occurs or is the case because things can develop in a certain way or because new things can come into being, which can then be in a certain way. For instance, it is possible that a future generation of human beings will be completely altruistic. But this seems possible only by virtue of the powers and potentialities future generations may have. Just imagine that future complete altruism is possible because every generation can train the next one to be more altruistic than it was itself. Then the possibility of a future generation being completely altruistic rests on the preceding generation's power to provide such altruistic training. The

27. Details vary; for an overview see Jacobs (2010, 236).

28. Vetter (2015, 18).

present generation does not therefore have a power to bring about a completely altruistic generation directly. The potential it does have is to raise a next generation which, in its turn, has the power to raise a next generation . . . which is completely altruistic. Possibility seems to require, in many instances, nested powers of this sort, and this is what is meant to be captured by the notion of "iterated potentialities."

There is, however, reason to doubt whether a scheme like POSSIBILITY will work as it stands. Can we really understand "potentialities for it to be the case that p" as genuine and actual properties of objects? They certainly look very different from ordinary powers to do things or to be in certain ways. This holds especially if the relevant p is not restricted to facts about the object itself, which, in Vetter's account, is not the case: I could have the potentiality for it to be the case that the Vesuvio erupts tomorrow, even though I have "nothing to do" with this volcano. Furthermore, it is doubtful whether *all* possibilities are "anchored" in potentialities of particular objects in this way. What about the statement "The laws of nature could have been very different"? This statement seems to be true, when the "could" is understood as expressing metaphysical , rather than physical possibility. But the statement doesn't just seem to be a statement about the potentialities, even iterated ones, of particular objects. Perhaps we have to posit something like "the whole universe" as the object that has the potentiality of being otherwise with regard to its natural laws, in order to dissolve this problem? This however would have the drawback of partly undermining the original motivation that made the explanation of possibility in terms of powers and potentialities attractive, namely to understand possibility in terms of how actual ordinary objects are.[29] This suggests that a scheme like POSSIBILITY cannot really explain *all* instances of metaphysical possibility, but, at best, part of them. Perhaps it can still be used to explain a more limited range of possibility, such as what it is metaphysically possible *for a given and existing object to do* (and even this more limited account would already be considerable philosophical progress). But precisely how this explanation will work is not obvious, since even if something has the power to do X, this power may still be masked (see chapter 2, section 2.5). So it seems that its being metaphysically possible for an object to do X cannot simply be equivalent to this object's having the power to do X. Thus the idea of the proposed analysis POSSIBILITY, even when applied to a restricted range of cases, may still need some refinement; but this is not to say that such refinement is not possible.

3.6 CONCLUSIONS

In this chapter we examined various attempts to account for necessity and possibility. We focused on *de re* necessity, namely the necessity that (supposedly) derives from essential properties of objects. In this context we examined Aristotle's essentialism, the relationship between essential and necessary properties, Quine's criticism of essentialism and the later revival of this theory. In the last part of the chapter we

29. Some philosophers would respond that the universe just is another ordinary object; Jonathan Schaffer has even argued that it is the only 'fundamental' object (2013). But clearly, the universe is not like the everday objects we ordinarily talk about.

looked for alternatives to the possible worlds model, which has been the standard approach to modal statements; and we explored the question of whether it would be possible to replace the latter with a semantics based on actual objects' powers.

*

4

CAUSALITY

4.1 INTRODUCTION

Things in the world change all the time. These changes (or most of them, anyway[1]) don't happen spontaneously, but because they are *caused* to occur. Since the beginning of rational thought, scientists and philosophers alike have considered it to be one of their main objectives to discover and understand the causes of changes in nature. Causation has therefore played a crucial role in nearly every attempt to make sense of the fabric of the world. Immanuel Kant, for instance, thought that causation was one of the necessary categories of thought by means of which we structure the different sensory impressions we have of the world, when we bring them into the order of one single and unified experience. Nearly two hundred years later, John Mackie captured the central importance of causation for our understanding of the world in his slogan that causation is the "cement of the universe" (1974); for causation, according to Mackie, is what holds together earlier and later stages in the history of the

1. Some people would argue that there are also changes which happen spontaneously: just on their own. But we can set the question of how such "uncaused changes" would work aside here.

universe, which would otherwise occur as unconnected bits and pieces, just one after the other. However, while nearly all philosophers agree on the crucial importance of causation, there is no consensus at all on how causation itself should be understood: what is it for *x* to cause *y*? Philosophers remain deeply divided on many hotly discussed issues in this regard, for instance (just to give you a glimpse of the debate): Is causation an irreducible primitive connection between entities, or can it be (explanatorily, or metaphysically) reduced to something else? What kind of entities stand in causal relations to one another: only events, or also substances? Or facts, rather than events? Only particular entities, or abstract entities as well? How is causation related to explanation? Is causation an extensional relation, which holds between two entities no matter how these entities are described, or an intentional one, which holds between entities only when they are described in particular ways?

Most of the modern debate on causation has been shaped by the influential empiricist tradition whose main historical proponent was David Hume, and which has attempted to reduce causation to the obtaining of (certain types of) regularities. As we have already seen in chapter 2 (section 2.4), Hume criticized the concept of causal power on the grounds that it failed to meet the empiricist criterion for meaningfulness which he advocated. This criterion required that we could trace back concepts to original impressions (as Hume puts it: all our ideas "are copied from impressions").[2] Inherently bound up with Hume's critique of the concept of power was his critique of the "traditional"

2. See *A Treatise of Human Nature*, 4, and *An Enquiry Concerning Human Understanding*, 9.

concept of causation. This is not surprising, because Hume considered the notion of "necessary connection," which on the traditional view was part and parcel of the notion of cause, as effectively synonymous to the notion of power.[3] The view that a cause is somehow necessarily connected to its effect—the cause "makes" its effect occur, and the effect "cannot help occurring" once the cause is active—is both intuitively appealing and has been historically highly influential. Causes, we normally think, make things happen, and this is what allows us to *explain* these effects by referring to their causes. But, Hume argued, we have no "original experience" of necessitation that could serve as the original experience to which the concept of causation could be traced back. Focusing on presumed causal connection between events (i.e., cases where presumably one event causes another one), Hume wrote:

> There is not, in any single, particular instance of cause and effect, anything which can suggest the idea of power or necessary connection. (*An Enquiry Concerning Human Understanding*, 63)

Hume thought that when we consider events or objects by themselves, and consider particular (supposed) instances of causation, we will never find any item in the world that would correspond to the idea of a causal nexus or a necessary connection. What we do observe is only that certain types of events are generally "conjoined": events of one type generally follow upon events of another type.

---

3. See *A Treatise of Human Nature*, 157.

> All events seem entirely loose and separate . . . one event
> follows another; but we can never observe any tie between
> them. They seem *conjoined*, but never *connected*. (*An Enquiry
> Concerning Human Understanding*, 74)

Having observed this conjunction on many occasions, when
we see an event of the first type we come to expect that an
event of the second type will follow. We then "project" or
reify in the world the connection we habitually make in our
minds, assuming that there is really something *out there*, in
the succession of events we observe, that links them together.
The source of our idea of causation is therefore, on Hume's
account, something merely subjective.

The projectivist or antirealist element of Hume's own
view—which claims that causation was "nothing real in the
world" but merely a projection of our minds—was, however, not as influential as the positive thesis about causation
that could be developed from Hume's arguments, namely,
that causation could be analyzed in terms of two other
ideas: (i) temporal succession and (ii) constant conjunction. Take Hume's own proposed "definition" of "cause" in
the *Enquiry*:

> A cause is an object, followed by another, where all objects
> similar to the first are followed by objects similar to the second.
> (*An Enquiry Concerning Human Understanding*, 76)

Or, to put this more precisely: for x to be a cause of y, (i) y has
to follow x in time and (ii) there must be a constant and reg-
ular pattern of items similar to y following upon items similar
to x. This proposal has three important implications for the
nature of causation, which are all far from uncontroversial,

but which have become key tenets of the Humean "orthodoxy" on causation.

First, cause and effect must be things that can "follow
one another," and, notwithstanding Hume's talk of "objects",
this best fits the case where one *event* causes another. By contrast, substances, which most of the philosophical tradition
prior to Hume had considered to be paradigmatic causes,
can rarely be said to "follow one another"—except in the
special sense in which descendants can be said to "follow"
their forebears, which is certainly not a model for standard
causal interactions. Nor is it the case that in normal causal
interactions an event temporally "follows" a substance: this
would require the substance to go out of existence before or
when the event occurs, which is, again, a rather exceptional
case. As a result, Humeans generally came to hold that the
causal relata are events rather than substances.

Second, on the Humean view, particular instances of
causation necessarily presuppose general regularities: for example, your pressing the light switch now can cause the light
to go on immediately afterward only if there is some general
regularity in play- whatever this may be. This regularity need
not connect events that we actually observe (perhaps you
have only turned this particular light switch on once in your
life); it may instead connect "hidden" intermediate steps between observable causes and effects. Still, on this view, there
can be no genuinely singularist causation, in the sense that
one individual event would cause another one *no matter
what else is going on in the world.* Third, on Hume's view we
can provide an analysis of causation in terms of elements that
are not themselves causal. Causal facts are completely determined by the non-causal facts in the world (i.e., the facts

about temporal succession and regularities). Once the latter facts are fixed, it is also fixed what causes what.

Contemporary Humeans mostly accept these three claims, even though they disagree with Hume with respect to the kind of general pattern that supposedly underlies individual instances of causation. Most contemporary neo-Humeans believe that such general patterns are not just regularities that hold *de facto*, but must be genuine laws of nature that support counterfactual statements. For this reason, their views are also called "nomological" views of causation. As they have shaped so much of the modern debate, nomological views of causation that follow Hume in rejecting singularist causation and in taking causal facts to be determined by non-causal facts, are a useful point of departure for our following discussion. In the next section (4.2), we will consider two influential more recent versions of the Humean approach, and examine some of the problems these accounts encounter. Such problems indicate that there are still major unresolved issues in the Humean approach. This motivates us to turn to Aristotle's account of causation (section 4.3), which will provide a useful foil for investigating how the shift toward realism with respect to powers that we have discussed in chapter 2 gives us new resources to account for causation in terms of the exercise of causal powers (section 4.4). In that context, we will also consider whether an account of causation in terms in powers can explain the direction of causation, by means of the distinction between active and passive powers. We will conclude the chapter by turning to the question of mental causation, that is, the question of how something mental can cause physical changes and vice versa (section 4.5).

4.2 SOME NEO-HUMEAN DEVELOPMENTS

As we have seen, contemporary Humeans tend to assume that the regularities that underlie particular causal connections are not just general regularities that hold as a matter of fact, but rather laws of nature. In taking this stance, neo-Humeans do not necessarily think of themselves as disagreeing with Hume; for he writes, directly after the definition of "cause" in the *Enquiry* quoted earlier: "Or, in other words, *where the first object had not been, the second never had existed*" (*An Enquiry concerning Human Understanding*, 76). These lines may suggest that Hume thought of causation not just as based on general regularities, but also in terms of necessary conditions.[4] The latter is a stronger conception, since some regularities are merely contingent. You can imagine, for instance, that, *de facto*, all men in a certain community put on their hats when going out. But this does not always warrant the conclusion that Jim, a man from that community, would not have gone out if he had not put on his hat. We can imagine that in a disaster scenario Jim would have to go out so urgently that he would do it even if he forgot his hat (even when such a situation *de facto* never occurs).

Many metaphysicians of neo-Humean allegiance endorse this stronger conception of causation, and take laws of nature to be the obvious candidates for what explains why a cause is necessary for its effect to occur. Their thought is that if there

---

4. At the same time, Hume's emphatic critique of the supposedly "necessary connection" involved in causation even more strongly suggests that he did want to settle for merely regularities. As a consequence, contemporary Humeans, while being generally inspired by him, can hardly claim to defend his own (historical) position.

is a law of nature such that an event of type A follows upon an event of type B, then we have a good explanation of why, *ceteris paribus*, if the B-type event had not occurred, the A-type event would not have occurred either. As a result, many neo-Humeans, from the nineteenth century onward, came to think of causes as necessary—or, going beyond Hume, necessary *and sufficient*—conditions for their effects (most notably John Stuart Mill). But this had the unwelcome effect of putting the philosophical analysis of causation very much at odds with our ordinary way of talking, both in everyday life and in scientific practice. For we ordinarily call many factors "causes" that are not, strictly speaking, necessary—or sufficient—for their effects. When we regard, for example, the throwing of a stone as the cause of the breaking of a window, the throwing of the stone might be neither necessary for the latter (since the window could have broken in many other ways as well) nor sufficient (since the window would not have broken had something arrested the stone in its flight). Presumably in most cases only very encompassing states of affairs involving the whole environment where a change takes place are truly sufficient or necessary for bringing about the effect; nonetheless we are prepared to call "causes" less encompassing factors too.

One of the most influential neo-Humean attempts to resolve this discrepancy between theory and (linguistic and scientific) practice is due to J. L. Mackie, who in his *The Cement of the Universe: A Study of Causation* (1974) tried to analyze the relation between particular causes and particular effects in terms of a sophisticated combination of necessary and sufficient conditions. As Mackie argued, a cause is not (normally) sufficient for its effects, nor is it necessary. To take Mackie's own example: a short circuit in a house causes a fire. The short circuit is not sufficient on its own to cause the fire, because without the presence of inflammable material and oxygen (etc.), the short circuit would not have brought about the fire. Neither is the short circuit necessary, since something other than the short circuit could in principle have caused the fire as well. Instead, Mackie claims, the short circuit is an Insufficient but Necessary part of a set of conditions which is itself Unnecessary but Sufficient for the effect. The cause of an effect is thus what he calls an **INUS** condition. The (overall) sufficient condition is a very large collection of contributory conditions that absolutely suffices for the effect on this occasion. Without the short circuit this collection of contributory conditions would not have sufficed for the effect though, and would not have led to the fire. Mackie's analysis therefore allows us to identify as causes factors that are by themselves neither necessary nor sufficient for the effect. At the same time, it captures the idea that in some respect (namely, under the conditions that actually obtained) the cause *was* necessary and sufficient for the effect. For given the other conditions, it was both. Thus, given the presence of the oxygen and of the inflammable material, as well as the absence of possible interferences that would have prevented the outbreak of the fire, the short circuit was sufficient for the outbreak of the fire. At the same time, given these other conditions and given that there was no other factor that would have led to the outbreak of the fire in combination with them, the short circuit was necessary for these other conditions to lead to the outbreak of the fire. We could therefore say that a cause is necessary and sufficient *under certain circumstances* for its effects. In limiting cases, Mackie admits, a cause may even be necessary and sufficient on its own: causes are, as he puts it, *at least* **INUS** conditions for their effects (1993, 36).

Mackie's proposed analysis has received a wide range of criticisms. These criticisms were in part inherited as criticisms of the original Humean analysis that Mackie was trying to refine, and in part specifically targeted at Mackie's own suggestions. Let us briefly consider here three difficulties that were raised against Mackie's account.

The first concerns the distinction between causes and background conditions. An obvious consequence of Mackie's analysis is that every event has many causes. (As we noted, this makes the analysis in one respect attractive.) For just as the short circuit is sufficient and necessary for its effects given the other circumstances (including the presence of oxygen), so the presence of oxygen is sufficient and necessary for its effects, given the other circumstances (including the short circuit). This generalizes to every other **INUS** condition of any effect. Some philosophers however resist the idea that things other than events (like the short circuit) are causes, and claim that other factors can only be "background" or "enabling" conditions. If they are right, Mackie's proposal, which rules out this distinction, has an obvious problem. However, in Mackie's defense, it must be pointed out that it is very hard to apply the "cause-*versus*-background condition" distinction to particular cases without stretching the facts to fit the theory, or making *ad hoc* stipulations. For instance, when we talk about "*the* cause of of the downfall of the Roman Republic", this ought not to be taken literally. The Roman Republic fell because of the defeat of the Republican Party in the Civil War, because of Caesar's ambition, because of the incompetence and corruption of the senators, but also because of the many unresolved longstanding tensions between the different social groups and the rise of new social classes (and you can add many other factors here). Is there any reason to think that only one of these is the *real* cause of the Republic's downfall, or that some of them are ? Why should we think, e.g., that the longstanding tensions cannot have been a proper cause, but only a background or "enabling" condition that facilitated the downfall? One may even be skeptical that an in-principle distinction between causes and background conditions has to be part and parcel of *any* viable theory of causation, for what we consider as background conditions—rather than causes—in each particular case depends, primarily, on our interests or expectations concerning the "normal state of affairs" in situations like the one at issue, and these expectations and interests change all the time. This suggests that the distinction between causes and background conditions is a pragmatic one, rather than a metaphysical one. Therefore, even if Mackie's theory has no good way to distinguish between background conditions and causes, this need not be a decisive objection against it.

A second difficulty raised against Mackie's account concerns the relation between causation and determinism. Mackie's account of causes as **INUS** conditions presupposes that there is a sufficient condition for the occurrence of the effect (even though this condition will encompass more than just individual causes taken singly). Positing sufficient conditions is unproblematic in cases of deterministic causation (i.e., where the effect *must* follow the cause). In nature however there are also cases of indeterministic causation, or so many believe, such as quantum mechanical processes (where the probability of the occurrence of the effect is significantly raised by the presence of the cause, but the effect is not necessitated). When an effect has only indeterministic causes, there will be no **INUS** conditions for this effect, simply because there is no set of previous conditions which ensured that this effect would take place. (Even a combination of causal factors, in such cases, merely raises the probability of the occurrence of the effect.) Mackie's conception of cause however rules out indeterministic causes from the start.

Finally, a third difficulty raised against Mackie's account concerns the direction of causation. It is usually thought that causation has a direction, "from" the cause "to" the effect. This directedness expresses itself in a formal feature of the causal relation, namely that it is nonsymmetric: if x causes y, this does not imply that y causes x (and in standard cases this won't be the case). One well-known challenge for those who attempt to define "cause" in terms of sufficient and necessary conditions is how to account for this directionality. Accounting for the directionality of causation is evidently a problem if one assumes that cause just is a necessary and sufficient condition for the effect—if x is necessary and sufficient for y, then it follows that y is necessary and sufficient for x. The general problem applies to accounts like Mackie's, because, as we saw, Mackie requires that if "A causes B" then A is *at least* an **INUS** condition for B, and allows that A can be necessary and sufficient for B on its own. The standard Humean way to account for the direction of causation is to use the direction of time (recall Hume's formulation: "followed by another"). But Mackie cannot appeal to the direction of time to underpin the directionality of causation, because he accepts the in-principle possibility of backward causation, where an event later in time causes an earlier event (1993, 51). Furthermore, this strategy does not work in cases of simultaneous causation, for here cause and effect happen at the same time.

David Lewis's theory of causation[5] promises to resolve at least the second and the third difficulty raised against

5. For Lewis's original views see the essays collected in his 1986b; for a critical reappraisal see his 2004.

Mackie's proposal. Lewis follows quite closely Hume's second definition of "cause": "where the first object had not been, the second never had existed," and provides a counterfactual analysis of (certain paradigmatic instances of) causation. As we saw in chapter 3, Lewis famously used the "toolbox" of possible worlds and the notion of comparative overall similarity of possible worlds to account for the truth conditions of counterfactual conditionals.

When "A $\square\rightarrow$ C" (see chapter 3, section 3.4.1) is true, then "C counterfactually depends on A."[6] Using this notion of counterfactual dependence, which is a relation between *propositions*, Lewis defines causal dependence, which is a relation between particular *events*. Assume that "c" and "e" are terms denoting particular events (e.g., "the assassination of the Archduke Ferdinand," "the outbreak of the First World War"); "O" is a predicate meaning "occurs;" and "~" is the negation sign. Causal dependence can then be defined as follows, so Lewis:

e causally depends on c iff:

(1) $Oc \square\rightarrow Oe$; and
(2) $\sim Oc \square\rightarrow \sim Oe$

If c and e are actual events, then (1) is always true because of the stipulation that the actual world is always the closest world to itself. Since c and e actually exist, there is a c-and-e world (i.e. a world in which both c and e exist) that is closer to actuality than any c-and-not-e world, because the actual world *is* a c-and-e world. And in *any* case of causation, the

---

6. For the version of Lewis's account and the terminology we are following here, see Lewis (1986b, chapter 21).

cause and the effect must actually exist. It is therefore clause (2) which is the real core of Lewis's counterfactual analysis of causation: it says that if *c* had not occurred, *e* would not have occurred.

Causal dependence is not the same as causation, though: Lewis says that causal dependence between actual events implies causation, but not *vice versa*. This is because causation is defined in terms of a chain of counterfactual dependence. A causal chain is defined as a sequence of actual events, *c*, *d*, *e* . . . and so on; where *d* depends on *c*, *e* depends on *d*, et cetera. Then *c* is a *cause* of *e* when there is a causal chain leading from *c* to *e*. Lewis's definitions allow that there could be a sequence where *a* causally depends on *b*; *b* causally depends on *c*; but *a* does not causally depend on *c*. Nonetheless, Lewis says, it will still be true that in this case *c* is a cause of *a*. Imagine, for instance, that Emma's mother woke her up this morning at 8 a.m., so that she would get the bus and get to her maths class on time. If Emma had not been woken up by her mother, she would not have been at the bus stop by 8:25 a.m., but only at 8:40 a.m., and would therefore not have caught the bus at 8:25 a.m.; and if she had arrived at the bus stop only at 8:40 a.m., there wouldn't have been another bus that would have got her to class on time. So, Emma's mother waking her up, by causing her to arrive at the bus stop in time, caused her to get to the class on time. But Emma could have come to the class on time even if her mother had not woken her up : for her father had already promised to give her a lift to school in his car for just that eventuality. His promise, however, had been restricted to the case in which Emma's mother would not have woken her up in time: once she did wake Emma up and Emma was on her way, her father was no longer available to pick her up from the bus stop and drive her to the class.[7] So, getting to the class on time did not causally depend on Emma's mother's waking her up early enough. Lewis thus defines causation as the *ancestral* of the relation of causal dependence. The ancestral of a relation R is that relation that stands to R as the relation of "being an ancestor" stands to the relation of "being a parent". The relation "being an ancestor of" can be roughly defined as follows: x is an ancestor of y if x is a parent of y, or x is a parent of a parent of y, or x is a parent of a parent of a parent of y . . . and so on. While "x is a parent of y" is not transitive (your grandmother is a parent of your parent, but not your parent herself), "x is an ancestor of y" is. The relations "x causally depends on y" and "x is a cause of y" have the same structure.

How does Lewis's proposal fare with regard to the second and third problems raised against Mackie's analysis? With regard to the second problem, Lewis's account is not committed to the idea that all causation must be deterministic. As long as we can make sense of comparative similarity in cases where only probabilistic connections between events are at stake, Lewis's analysis of causation will work for such cases too. With regard to the third problem, to account for direction of causation in a way that does not just posit that the direction of causation is the direction of time, Lewis has tried to show (from considerations about comparative similarity among possible worlds) that the analysis of counterfactual dependence gives us a principled reason to pick the direction of time. (The key idea, which we cannot go into in detail here, is that in our world events have more effects than

---

7. This part of the example is important because it ensures that Emma's being at the bus stop in time was, under the circumstances, necessary for her getting to her maths class in time.

causes; and that as a result worlds with the same or very similar pasts are bound to be more similar to one another than worlds with the same futures.) Not everyone however has been persuaded by this answer to the third difficulty raised against Mackie's account. It is also noteworthy that Lewis's response does not work for cases of simultaneous causation (where the direction of causation *cannot* be the direction of time).

However, Lewis's proposal faces some other problems. To begin with, there seem to be many cases of counterfactual dependence between events that are not cases of causation or causal dependence (see, e.g., Kim 1993). Assume, for instance, that Jim has promised Jane not to drink alcohol tonight, and this was the only promise Jim has ever made to Jane. If Jim did drink alcohol tonight, he thereby broke a promise to Jane. Also, given that this was his only promise to Jane, if he hadn't drunk alcohol tonight, he wouldn't have broken a promise to her. So both conditions for causal dependence, in Lewis's analysis, are satisfied. But Jim's drinking alcohol didn't *cause* him to break a promise to Jane: his drinking *constituted* a breaking of his promise. Generalizing this point, philosophers like Jaegwon Kim have objected to Lewis's account that causation is only one of many kinds of dependence relation that can underlie the counterfactual conditionals which Lewis takes to be the core of causal dependence. So how can we pick *causal* dependence relations out of the many possible dependence relations? (If we want to provide an analysis of causation that is not circular, we obviously cannot use the criterion that it is a dependence that rests on causal connections!)

In addition, there are some types of case involving causation that Lewis's analysis does not seem to cover, in particular cases of causal overdetermination and pre-emption. In over-determination cases, there are two sufficient causes, such that each of them could be absent (singly), and the effect would still obtain. Assume, for instance, that two assassins, independently from each other, shoot President Kennedy, such that their bullets enter his heart at exactly the same time. Arguably in such a case, if the first assassin had not fired, the second would still have killed President Kennedy. The same applies, *mutatis mutandis*, to the second assassin. So none of their shots was necessary, and for each the counterfactual "If the shot had not been fired, the President would not have died" is false. Nonetheless, we would usually consider both shots as causes of the President's death.[8]

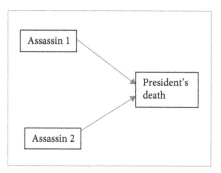

Pre-emption cases are trickier. In pre-emption cases, event A causes event B, but if A had failed to obtain or to have a causal influence, there would have been a "back-up" cause C that would have caused B anyway. In such cases, where A preempts C from causing the effect B, even if A is a cause of B, B would still have obtained if A had been absent.

8. Lewis did not want to address these cases because, as he put it, he lacks "firm naïve opinions about them" (1986b, 171 fn. 12). Many philosophers however find these cases compelling and have strong intuitions about them.

Imagine that one of the two assassins shoots the President, hits his mark and kills him instantaneously. The second assassin was there as a "back-up," and fired his shot two seconds after the first, to ensure the death of the President in case the first assassin's bullet had gone astray. Let us assume that the second assassin was a dead-certain shot, and his bullet would have certainly killed the President; however, when it reached him, the President was already dead (since the first bullet had been lethal). In this case clearly it was the first assassin's shot that killed the President (since the second assassin's bullet arrived too late). Nonetheless, it isn't true that if the first assassin hadn't shot, the President wouldn't have died (for in that case the second assassin's bullet would have killed him). Thus the counterfactual analysis is incorrect in concluding that the first assassin's shot did *not* cause the President's death.

Lewis's own response to pre-emption cases appeals to his definition of causation in terms of a chain of causally dependent events. The first assassin's shot causes the President's death because there is a chain of events between this shooting and the death (the bullet flying out of the gun and through the air, hitting the President's heart, etc.). Each event in this chain is causally dependent on the one before, but this does not mean that the death is causally dependent on the shooting (remember the case of Emma going to her maths class). So, the fact that there is a back-up does not prevent the shot from causing the death. However, this response strategy works only when the pre-emption case involves a chain of intermediate causal steps, and the pre-empted factor it not responsible for (some of) the earlier steps . But could there not be preemption just at the very last (or the only) step in a chain? Imagine, for instance, that a magician can cause the President's death by casting a spell. If the magician casts the spell immediately before the bullet hits the President, and by doing this directly kills the President, the only cause of the President's death is the spell, not the bullet (which arrives too late to kill the President). Nonetheless, that the bullet was already underway made it necessary that the President would die anyway. This seems to be a case of pre-emption not amenable to Lewis's response strategy, since the causal chain from spell to death involves no further intermediate steps, and causal dependence does not hold with regard to the single step in the chain which led to the death (i.e. from the magician's casting the spell to the President's death).

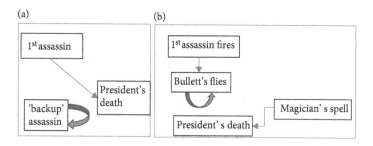

Even refined neo-Humean theories such as Mackie's and Lewis's thus face serious difficulties (of which we have been able to discuss only a very small selection here). Such difficulties have motivated a shift of interest among metaphysicians: an increasing number of philosophers have come to think that these difficulties make it worthwhile to look back at the Aristotelian conception of causation that Hume had tried to discredit, and are exploring whether it might be fruitful to start afresh from there. This is what we will do in the following two sections of this chapter too.

4.3 ARISTOTLE'S THEORY
OF CAUSATION

. Aristotle famously distinguished four types of cause.[9] Take a
particular statue made by Fidias, the statue of Athena on the
Acropolis in Athens. Aristotle's view is that the marble from
which it is made is its *material* cause; the form (of Athena) is
its *formal* cause; Fidias who sculpted it, its *efficient* cause; and
the purpose for which it was made, for example, to adorn the
Acropolis, its *final* cause. Today we find it somewhat awk-
ward to talk of each of these four things as "causes," because
we have become accustomed to reserving the term "cause" to
the third kind of Aristotelian causes, namely efficient causes
(and regard the other things as "explanatory factors" only).
This awkwardness is however mostly due to the fact that
our conception of causation radically changed in the seventeenth century, as part of the rise of the natural sciences and
their explanatory paradigms . For Aristotle , by contrast, as
well as for other philosophers of antiquity and the middle
ages, there are more types of cause than the efficient cause;[10]
Aristotle considers the material, efficient , formal and final
ones as being all genuine causes , for which there should be a
unified metaphysical account. The account he offers , simply
put, is that all causes are (related to) powers, and causation,
of all kinds, is the exercise or manifestation of mutually dependent causal powers. The mutual dependence among
powers is grounded in the fact that for Aristotle they are
(monadic) properties of a special type that he calls "relatives".

9. This section draws on Marmodoro (2007).

10. See, e.g., Sorabji (1980, 26–44); Frede (1987, 125–50).

The relevant powers are mutually dependent not for their existence but for their exercise: any agent requires a patient upon which to act.

To get a better idea of this theory, let us focus on the analysis Aristotle gives of the causal interaction (of the efficient causation type) between mover and movable in his discussion of *kinesis* (change, motion) in *Physics* III. Aristotle's definition of motion (see, e.g., 201a9–10; 201a27–9; 201b4–5; 202a13–4) is fairly broad[11] and includes what we would consider uncontroversial and paradigm instances of causation, such as building, heating, and doctoring. Thus, Aristotle's account of the mover-movable interaction will serve as a good model for explicating more generally his metaphysics of causation. What are the key elements of a causal interaction such as the one existing between a mover and a moved? Aristotle begins with a programmatic statement: accounting for motion does not require appealing to any new, primitive category of being (*Physics* 200b32–201a3); instead, Aristotle will use some of the key ideas he has introduced elsewhere without adding anything more to his ontological "stock" in order to explain motion and change. These key ideas are: forms, the privation of form, the substratum of change, and the distinction between being in potentiality and being in actuality. He describes efficient causation as the "transmission" of a form from the mover to the movable:[12]

---

11. Aristotle's definition allows for a great variety of cases to come under the mover–movable relation, including such cases as aging, which we would consider as untypical cases of causation at best.

12. This is, however, as we will see in a moment, only a figurative description; there is no item that gets literally passed on.

> The mover will always transmit a form, either a "this" or such
> or so much, which, when it moves, will be the principle and
> cause of the motion, e.g. the actual man begets man from what
> is potentially man. (*Physics* 202a9–12)

So in general terms, in causal interactions between substances
the agent transmits and the patient receives the form; the
same form is involved "on both sides," only that they relate to this form differently. The agent's transmitted form is
the cause; the privation of the form in the patient is what
allows for its reception, and the physical process facilitating
the transmission of the form is the *substratum* of the causal
change (e.g., in building, the movements of the hands of the
builder facilitate the transmission of the form of the house to
the construction materials; for heating, contact facilitates the
transmission of the form to the object heated). Describing
(figuratively) causation in terms of "transmission of the form"
plays an important role in Aristotle's account of causation. In
particular, it enables him to address the question of whether
causation follows the order of time, with causes preceding
their effects. If not, is it mere convention that in the causal
interaction between the teacher and the pupil, teaching is the
cause and learning the effect? Or is there an underlying metaphysical principle for the determination of the cause and
the effect? Aristotle writes,

> A man may have hearing and yet not be hearing, and that
> which has sound is not always sounding. But when that
> which can hear is actively hearing and that which can sound
> is sounding, then the actually hearing and the actual sound
> come about *at the same time* (these one might call respec-
> tively hearkening and sounding). (*De Anima* 425b26–426a1,
> emphasis added)

Aristotle is thus clear that actual causes do not precede their actual effect in time; teaching and learning (by being taught) occur during the same time span. The passage just quoted also shows that Aristotle conceives of causation as the exercise of causal powers that get mutually activated: the power of sounding in the example, and of hearing. In *Physics* III 3, Aristotle further specifies these points: the power to teach is in the teacher before she engages in actual teaching (and even if she may never engage in actual teaching), and so is the corresponding passive power in the learner; but the actualization of these potentials is one and the same, hence there is complete overlap in time between them.[13] Aristotle goes on to give a metaphysical account of this key claim that the actualization of the active and the passive powers is *one and the same*, which is what also explains their temporal coincidence. He writes:

> Motion is the fulfillment of the potentiality of the movable by the action of that which has the power of causing motion . . . A thing is capable of causing motion because it can do this, it is a mover because it actually does it. But it is on the movable that is capable of acting. *Hence there is a single actuality of both of them alike.* (*Physics* 202a13–18, emphasis added)

Aristotle's claim will look, at first sight, puzzling, but he explicates it when he examines some alternative accounts of what happens to the mover and the movable in causation in a dialectical puzzle immediately following the passage just quoted, at 202a21–b5.[14] In the course of this discussion,

13. It is important to note, though, that this complete overlap does not raise problems for accounting for the direction of causation. For the direction of the transmission of the form is asymmetric, and that determines which is the agent and which the patient in the causal interaction.

14. See Marmodoro (2007, 207, 230–31).

Aristotle rejects some of the possible alternatives to the claim that the actualization of both powers is one and the same, while developing the rationale behind his own explanation of the "oneness" of agency and patiency. Aristotle considers two main possibilities: that the two actualities, of the mover and the movable, are different; or that they are one and the same. The first option seems to lead to a dilemma. If the two actualities are different, either they both occur in one of the two subjects (namely, either in the mover or the moved); or one occurs in each. If both actualities occur in one subject, then whichever has both actualities in it will change at the same time in two different ways in relation to one form. For example, when we take the case of A teaching B, then one person would come to be both teaching and learning at the same time by teaching, and this, to Aristotle, seems absurd (we can follow him in this assessment if we exclude those cases where someone teaches herself). If on the other hand the actuality of the mover is in the mover, and the actuality of the movable is in the movable, then either the causal agency of the mover will impact only on the mover itself, and not on the movable (so the teacher will teach herself, but not the pupil), or it will impact on nothing (the teacher will teach nobody), in which case the mover is not a mover in actuality. Given that the assumption that the actualities are different leads to untenable results, it appears that the actualities cannot be different and must be one and the same. But this latter result is no less *prima facie* absurd, because agency and patiency cannot be the same. Aristotle's solution is that the two actualizations, of the agent's and of the patient's respective powers, are different, but also one, because interdependent, and they both take place in the patient. Immediately after developing the dilemma we just examined, Aristotle states his own position on the issue:

> Nor is it necessary that the teacher should learn, even if to act and be acted on are one and the same, provided that they are not the same in respect of the account [*logos*] which states their essence [*to ti ên einai*] (as raiment and dress), but are the same in the sense in which the road from Thebes to Athens and the road from Athens to Thebes are the same, as has been explained above. (*Physics* 202b10–14)

Thus, for Aristotle, even if both actualities are in one sense the same, they are different "in respect of their *logos.*" There has been much discussion in the literature concerning how to understand this last crucial term, *logos*, but the context makes it clear that it must refer to the definition of the respective natures. For Aristotle uses in the passage the technical expression he has coined for essence (*to ti ên einai*, which we already know from the discussion of Aristotle's essentialism in section 3.2.). One might think that reading *logos* this way makes Aristotle's position even more puzzling. For it is a cornerstone of Aristotle's essentialism that if the essences of two things are of different kinds (say a wolf and a rabbit), the two things in question must be essentially and numerically different. What it is to be an agent is different from what it is to be a patient; their definitions are different (202a20, 202b22), and with them, their kind (202b1). Nonetheless, although the definitions stating their essences are different, Aristotle maintains, "to act and to be acted on are one and the same" (202b11). The example he offers helps us to better understand what he means by this. The route from Athens to Thebes and the route from Thebes to Athens are in a sense "one and the same", for these routes are embodied in the same stretch of the road. In the same way, the ground of the respective actualizations of agency and patiency is one and the same, notwithstanding that agency and patiency are actualizations of essentially different powers. Aristotle states this explicitly when he writes:

> To generalize, teaching is not the same in the primary sense with learning, nor is agency with patiency, but that to which those belong [*scilicet*] is the same for both, namely the motion; for the actualization of this [teaching] in that [learning] and the actualization of that [learning] through the action of this [teaching] differ in definition. (*Physics* 202b19–22)

The two powers or potentialities in question differ in type, thus their actualities too differ in type. But the actualities of the two potentialities (for teaching and for learning) are realized in the motion that is the common activity that actualizes them both. The two potentialities can thus occur in actuality only together, and neither can happen without the other. The teacher is not teaching if the learner is not learning, and the learner (i.e., instructee) is not learning (being instructed) if the teacher is not teaching. The oneness of the activity grounding them accounts for the interdependent actualization of the cause and the effect. At the same time, the two essences or forms that the activity bears preserve the bipolarity of the causal interaction. Lastly, as we will see in the next section, the fact that the activity that actualizes both agency and patiency is located in the patient grounds the distinction between agent and patient, and between the active and passive powers which are involved in the causal "transaction".

4.4 ARE THERE *ACTIVE* AND *PASSIVE* POWERS INVOLVED IN CAUSATION?

Aristotle's view discussed in the previous section has many attractive features. And, as we have noted at the end of section 4.2, the problems which neo-Humean accounts of causation still face have motivated a growing number of philosophers to look back to Aristotle's model of causation, and to endorse at least some crucial elements of it. Contemporary neo-Aristotelians do believe that one can provide an account of causation in terms of the actualization of potentialities (as Aristotle would have put it) or the exercise of powers (as we would put it). This Aristotelian idea, they hold, allows us to revive the idea that causation involves "production," and that the effects "derive" from their causes, which had been lost by the Humean tradition (Anscombe 1993, 92). Different approaches to developing this idea have been tried out; they can be classified in different ways. One important distinction depends on whether causation is accounted for in terms of the coming together or "coactivation" of different powers, active and passive; or whether causation need involve the manifestation of one kind of power only, namely an active power.[15] Another important distinction can be drawn according to what these approaches take the relata of causation to be: powers, events, or objects? Yet another distinction can be drawn according to whether one believes that all instances of causation, or

15. For the first view see, e.g., Marmodoro (2007) and Mumford and Anjum (2011); for the second, O'Connor (2009) and Mayr (2011).

only some, can be understood in terms of the activation of powers.[16]

Many—but not all—power theories of causation adopt the distinction between active and passive powers in some form or other. What makes this move attractive is that it promises to provide an explanation for the direction of causation, which, as we have seen in section 4.2, raises special difficulties for the neo-Humeans. Some philosophers though have rejected the distinction between agent and patient in causal transactions, and argued that all causal transactions are symmetrical, in the sense that all causal partners undergo changes. Take for instance the following passage by John Heil:

> The received view of causation might lead you to think that the water and the salt are related as agent and patient: the water, or maybe the water's enveloping the salt, causes the salt to dissolve. Perhaps the water possesses an "active power" to dissolve salt, and salt a complementary "passive power" to be dissolved by water. But look more closely at what happens when you stir salt into a glass of water. Certain chemical features of the salt interact with certain chemical features of the water. . . . This interaction is, or appears to be, continuous, not sequential; it is, or appears to be, symmetrical. (Heil 2012, 118)

16. In the literature, this last question is sometimes dealt with under the heading of whether all kind of causation is of one kind, e.g., substance-causation (Lowe 2002), or whether there are irreducibly different kinds of causation, e.g., some kinds where causation consists in the activation of a causal power of a substance and others which run along more or less Humean lines. Some so-called agent-causalists in the free-will debate go for the latter option, e.g., O'Connor (2000) and Clarke (1996).

Much-discussed cases, that seem to display this symmetry in a particularly striking way, are that of two cards leaning against one another and sustaining each other in their position (Heil 2017), and that of an icecube cooling a drink in a glass while being itself warmed up (and melted) (Mumford/ Anjum 2011, 120). Cases such as the two mutually sustaining cards are very common in nature and show, according to Heil, that there is no real metaphysical distinction between agent and patient, and hence between the manifestation of active and passive powers. There is only one single manifestation of both, the fact that we call it "dissolving" or "being dissolved" (in the case of salt in water) is a perspectival matter based on how we look at events and what we are interested in.

Heil's argument is not compelling though. Let us grant that there are some cases of symmetrical interactions, like the case of the two cards leaning against one another. It would be hasty to infer from that *all* cases of causation are like that. Let us return to our original case of the water dissolving the salt. Even if both the salt and the water change during the process, Heil's claim that the interaction is fully symmetrical is unwarranted. For there are still important differences between what the salt and the water do to each other. For instance, polarized water molecules break the bond between the negative chloride ions and the positive sodium ions, while salt molecules do not break any water molecule. The chemical reaction is asymmetrical. The fact that water dissolves salt but not *vice versa* is scientifically explicative: if we say that water dissolves salt we are communicating scientific knowledge, and more specifically knowledge about the relevant causal process.

What then differentiates active and passive powers, if their distinction is what underpins the asymmetry and directionality of causality? Their distinction can either be thought to be an absolute one, such that a power is (generally, by nature) either a passive or an active one; or a relative one, such that powers take on an active or passive role in causation depending on how they are involved in the interaction, as Aristotle for instance thought. For Aristotle, a power is active if it causes a change in another power or its bearer; and is passive if it or its bearer undergoes change. (Even if two powers or bearers change, one can change more or more radically than the other, as in the example of water and salt; so we can still compare degrees of undergoing or causing change.) An alternative way to distinguish between active and passive powers focuses on the (relative) dependence of the manifestation of a power on the external circumstances. A power is comparatively more active, on this view, the wider the variety of circumstances under which it *can* manifest, and the smaller the variety of circumstances under which it *has to* manifest. This is one way to capture the idea that causation is tightly connected to the explanatory contribution something makes to an effect, and this explanatory contribution is relatively greater for a power if the relative explanatory contribution of the external circumstances is relatively smaller.[17] In both suggested ways of distinguishing active from passive powers, it is important to note that the distinction between active and passive is not merely based on epistemological or pragmatic considerations, but on metaphysical ones.[18]

17. See, e.g., Harré and Madden (1975); Mayr (2011, chap. 8).

18. The distinction between active and passive powers in a causal interaction might not be easy or unequivocal in certain cases. However, this doesn't mean that the distinction in general makes no sense.

4.5 MENTAL CAUSATION

It seems a trivial truism that mental occurrences can have causal effects; and equally it seems obviously true that mental occurrences can cause not only other mental occurrences, but physical ones as well. Imagine yourself thinking hard about the solution to a mathematical problem ("What is 246 + 874?") and suddenly grasping the solution ("Ah, it's 1120!"). Your thinking "Ah, it's 1120!" is a mental event. It can not only cause you to have other thoughts (e.g., "So the overall sum is 5698"), but can also have physical effects (e.g., your writing down "1120" on your exam sheet). Or imagine yourself feeling a sharp pang of pain as you touch an extremely hot cup of tea. Wouldn't we naturally assume that it is your pain that causes you to cry out loud? Also, when you intend to do something, this intention, it seems, can clearly impact causally on what you are doing: unless you are weak-willed or somehow prevented, your intention will make you act in certain ways.[19] These three cases, and others like it, seem to be clear cases of causation. So it seems obvious that mental occurrences can have both mental and physical effects.

Nonetheless, since the time of Descartes the problem of mental causation has been haunting metaphysicians. In Descartes's own system the problem arises from his mind–body dualism, which includes a strict distinction between

19. It is disputed whether this is best understood as your intention causing you to act in certain ways. But because we do not follow the traditional picture of event-causation here, we will set this problem aside, because the intention can at least manifest itself in your actions, which is enough for its being causally relevant.

purely mental entities (souls), characterized by the property of being conscious, and physical entities (bodies), which do not have any mental properties. Descartes's dualism made the question of how these two types of substance, mind and body, could interact particularly pressing for him—while his philosophical assumptions made this question almost unanswerable. To begin with, the mind was for Descartes not localized in any part of the body, which left it completely mysterious how it could impact on the latter. Famously Descartes thought that there was a specific organ in the body, the pineal gland, that allowed the soul to act upon the body; but positing that there was such an organ hardly solved the general problem of how a purely mental entity could interact at all with another object completely different from it. (Several philosophers despaired that providing an answer to this question was possible; most notably Malebranche, who thought that every apparent interaction between soul and body was mediated by divine intervention. This view is known as "occasionalism".)

The problem of mental causation as it arose for Descartes was directly tied to his view of substance dualism: that is, the view that mental and physical substances formed two exclusive kinds of substances that did not share any of their essential properties. Substance dualism has become very much a minority position today, and its demise has largely been due to its inability to explain causal interactions between mind and body. Nowadays, most philosophers accept some form of physicalism, according to which—minimally—*all* there is in the doman of the natural world are physical entities with physical properties. But the problem of mental causation has returned in different forms—and presumably, as long as mental and physical items (be they substances, properties, or events) are considered to form exclusive sets, this problem will keep haunting philosophers in some form or other.[20] Even if one believes that all substances are physical substances, one will still have to assume that some of these substances have mental properties and states, and are subject to mental occurrences too. We human beings, for instance, have mental properties and states: we have beliefs and desires; we sometimes feel joy, or acute pangs of pain. How are these properties, states, and occurrences related to our physical properties and states, and the physical events in which we are involved?

One way to answer this question is to hold that mental properties and physical properties are identical; that is, that for every mental property P there is a physical property P* (which may be a highly complex one), such that P is identical with P*, and that instantiating P is the same as instantiating P*. If so, there is no longer any specific problem of mental causation: if mental properties were identical with physical properties, their causal relevance would be explained just in the very same terms as the causal relevance of other physical properties. This view is held by reductive materialists—but it is not a view that many contemporary philosophers subscribe to. Influential arguments (such as Hilary Putnam's [1975] *multiple realization* argument that the same mental states can be realized by many different physical set-ups)

---

20. What makes an event or property a mental or a physical one? This question is a tricky one and not all participants in the debate give the same answer. Two features that have often been used to characterize mental items are consciousness (Descartes) or intentionality (Brentano). We will use the following as a rough-and-ready characterization: X is a mental property/event/state if it essentially involves either consciousness or intentionality.

have convinced most that mental and physical properties cannot be identical. If the properties are not identical though, then types of mental states cannot be identical to types of physical states either, and being in mental state S cannot be exactly the same thing as being in physical state S*. For, plausibly, being in a certain state is (at least in part) defined as instantiating a certain property or standing in a certain relation, such that two states cannot be identical to one another unless the properties involved are also the same. Given that most philosophers , while rejecting reductive materialism, still subscribe to a version of physicalism, their views are usually called versions of "non-reductive physicalism".[21]

Non-reductive physicalism is, arguably, the mainstream position in philosophy of mind today. But if mental and physical properties/events/states are not regarded as identical, the problem of mental causation rears its head again. One of the most influential contemporary versions of the problem has been formulated by Jaegwon Kim, with his so-called *exclusion argument* (1998, 30), which targets specifically non-reductive physicalists. Physicalists, says Kim, must assume that there is some connection between physical and mental properties, and one widely accepted way to think about this connection is in terms of supervenience. While there are different notions of supervenience, the core idea is that properties of type A supervene on properties of type B if there can be no difference in the A-type properties of

21. Of course there are other options in addition to believing that mental and physical properties are identical or believing they are fully separate. You might, for instance, think that one and the same property has both mental and physical aspects. But we will set these further options aside here.

an object, state, or event, without some difference in the B-type properties, either of the object, state, or event itself or its "surroundings," or history. Such a supervenience assumption is very common, for example, with regard to the relation between moral and nonmoral properties: two actions cannot differ in their moral evaluation, it is widely assumed, unless there is some nonmoral difference between them as well. The same, Kim argues, can also be supposed to hold with regard to mental and physical properties:

> Mental properties *supervene* on physical properties, in that necessarily any two things (in the same or different possible worlds) indiscernible in all physical properties are indiscernible in mental respects. (Kim 1998, 10)

Thus the instantiation of any mental properties must have an underlying "basis" in the instantiation of some physical properties, which is usually called the "supervenience base". By itself, the supervenience thesis does not imply any claim that the physical properties are more basic than the mental ones. But most of the philosophers Kim's argument was originally intended to address, being physicalists, would also accept that the physical properties are more fundamental, and that it is due to their instantiation that the mental properties are instantiated as they are (and not *vice versa*).

A second key assumption of the *exclusion argument* is the thesis of the causal closure of the physical realm. While there are different formulations of this thesis, the core idea is that the causal laws that govern the physical realm only allow for causation of physical events by other physical events, since for every physical event there is we can already provide a full causal explanation of it in terms of physical causes. Kim holds that this assumption of causal closure is another key tenet of physicalism that one cannot give up as long as one subscribes to at least a weak form of physicalism:

> If you reject this principle, you are ipso facto rejecting the . . . completability of physics—that is, the possibility of a complete and comprehensive physical doctrine of all physical phenomena. . . . It is safe to assume that no serious physicalist could accept such a prospect. (Kim 1998, 40)

It is not difficult to see that these background assumptions (that physical properties are fundamental and there is causal closure of the physical realm) generate a fundamental difficulty for the possibility of mental causation. Let us begin with the question of whether on this picture mental events can cause physical effects. The answer is clearly in the negative. If one reads the causal closure principle as excluding nonphysical causes for physical effects, it directly rules out this possibility. But even if one gives the principle a weaker formulation (that is, allowing for the existence, in principle, of nonphysical causes in addition to physical ones), causation of physical effects by mental causes will be highly problematic: for, by causal closure, the physical effects will already have physical causes; so what work is there left for the mental causes to do? To make matters worse, when the mental event appears as a putative cause of a physical event, there will be an obvious contender for the former's causal role, namely the (physical) supervenience base of this mental event. All causal influence that the mental event could have will necessarily reduce to the influence of this physical base—or so it seems. The case of mental-to-mental causation appears, at first, more promising, since the closure principle doesn't tell us anything about the causes of mental events. However, as Kim argued, even here there is fundamental problem. When a mental event A causes another mental event B, B will also—according to the supervenience thesis principle—have a physical supervenience base B*. And, when B supervenes on B*, Kim claimed, it is plausible to assume that one can only cause B by causing its supervenience base to obtain, that is, by causing B* to obtain. But since the obtaining of B* is a physical event, A's causing B* would be a case of mental-to-physical causation—and, as the first part of the argument showed, this kind of causation is ruled out by the causal closure principle. If we take this principle seriously, we will not take A to be the genuine cause of B* (and, by extension, of B itself), but, instead, A's supervenience base A*. Could one, however, not say that both A and A* cause B, because A* causes B *via* causing A? "No", Kim argued, because the supervenience relation is not a causal relation. Thus we do not have a causal chain going from A* *via* A to B* and B; we only have a direct causal link from A* to B*. Attributing any causal role to A, such as a direct causal link between A and B, would be superfluous. In addition, it would make the case one of causal overdetermination, where B would have two distinct causal antecedents which would both fully explain its occurrence. It is not attractive to think of all putative cases of mental causation as cases of causal overdetermination, where the effect would occur even if the mental event itself was causally inert.

Kim's argument has encountered strong criticism—unsurprisingly, since, if successful, it would undermine too much of our commonsense picture of the world. Indeed, it would not only render mental causation impossible (which would be bad enough). It would also undermine practically all ordinary causal explanations, where macro-physical phenomena that are taken to supervene on microphysical phenomena are cited as causes (see, e.g., Humphreys 1997). Surely, we do not think that ordinary causal explanations such as "The rise in temperature caused the plants to whither" are all false, even though we do think there are underlying microphysical phenomena (of which we yet lack full understanding) on which the rise in temperature and the withering of the plants supervene. Having to reject all such ordinary explanations would be hardly an acceptable option and this in itself gives us strong reasons for rejecting at least one of the premises Kim uses in his argument (e.g., Baker 1993). But which part of the setup of Kim's argument should we deny? One might, of course, deny non-reductive physicalism in the first place. But given the latter's popularity, the premise that has usually been taken to be most problematic is the causal closure assumption. Why should we think that physical effects must have only physical causes, or that they must at least have a full causal history given in terms of physical causes only? We may have independent reasons for accepting some form of supervenience, but causal closure is not an intuitively plausible principle, since it clashes with many of our ordinary causal explanations, where we do explain physical effects by appeal to causes falling outside the purview of physics (but inside the purview of, e.g., chemistry or biology). Indeed, considering how the causal closure premise eventually leads us to deny (as long as we accept supervenience) that any phenomena other than microphysical phenomena can be causally effective, it is even doubtful that the robust "realism about science" that is meant to motivate the principle (and which Kim clearly endorses; see preface of his Kim [1998]) really supports it. For such a realism about science should lead us to be realist about the subject matters of *all* the sciences, *not just microphysics*. At least the other natural sciences, such as organic chemistry and biology, should, even for naturalist philosophers, be above doubt. Of course, one might still worry about how the processes and events specified in these different sciences causally interact; so there is still *some* question to be answered here. But Kim's argument is specifically based on scientific realism, and derives from this that mental causation is *impossible* (not just problematic). If we are genuine realists about science, and not simply realists about microphysics only, this argument cannot work, for there will be no reason to believe that in principle only explanations of events in terms of causally effective microphysical processes can be sound causal explanations. A more liberal naturalism that takes all the sciences seriously, will then be a more promising version of the physicalism than the the version Kim subscribes to, which is too deeply rooted in the reductionist programs of the first half and mid-twentieth century, which tried to find a common basis for all the sciences in physics. If such a more liberal naturalism is incompatible with causal closure and supervenience, and causal closure is the more dubious of the two premises, then all the worse for causal closure!

There is also another consideration that speaks strongly against the causal closure principle that Kim proposes, namely that when we focus on event causation, causes should be "proportional" to their effects (e.g., Yablo 1992).[22] The idea behind this "proportionality" response to Kim is the following: when we ask "What caused x?", we do not

---

22. Yablo (1992, 227) argues that usually, among the various candidates for the cause of an effect, the most proportional candidate should be preferred.

always want to know the most specific factor that can be picked out; rather, we want to know the factor that "made the difference", and this can be a relatively coarse-grained one. Imagine for instance that you are wearing a crimson red t-shirt and a bull, on seeing the t-shirt, gets angry and charges you. What caused the bull's anger? In some sense, obviously, your crimson t-shirt having the color it had. However, your t-shirt is not just crimson; it has a particular shade of crimson, for example, dark crimson. Its being crimson supervenes on its having this particular shade (it could not have had another color without some change with respect to this shade) and, in a way, its being crimson is due to its having that shade. Nonetheless, in response to the question of what caused the bull to be angry, it would be wrong to single out the t-shirt's specific shade as the causal factor. For the bull would have gotten angry *regardless of which particular shade of crimson your t-shirt had*: its being crimson was all it took for the bull to get angry. So, it was the t-shirt's being crimson that made the difference to the bull's getting angry, not its having the particular shade of crimson it had.

This shows that sometimes it is the supervenient property that makes the difference and is rightly singled out as the cause, rather than its supervenience base. Even if every instantiation of a mental property is supposed to have a physical supervenience base, it might therefore still be the instantiation of the mental property that makes the difference, rather than the instantiation of the physical property that underlies it. When one supervenient mental property instantiation can have different physical supervenience bases, it might be completely irrelevant to the occurrence of an effect which of these different bases was instantiated in the particular case under consideration . The only relevant factor is that the mental property was instantiated, regardless of what its underlying base was in the circumstances.

There are therefore several possible ways to respond to Kim's *exclusion argument*. There are even more options if we adopt a power-based view of causation of the sort we have discussed in sections 4.3. and 4.4. As we have seen in chapter 2, powers are at least partly individuated by what they are powers to do (i.e., their characteristic manifestations). At the same time, that a power's manifestation includes a physical effect does not automatically mean that the power is a purely physical, nonmental one. For the conditions for its exercise, or its exercise itself, may essentially involve mental elements too. You have the power to bring about a physical effect in the world—for example to move your arm. Need this power be a physical one? Not necessarily, especially if we take the rough-and-ready criterion of "mental" that X is a mental property if it essentially involves consciousness or intentionality.[23] For your power might be a power to move your arm as you want to: then its exercise would essentially involve intentionality and the power would thus count as a mental power. Nonetheless, the effect of the manifestation of this power is something physical: that your arm moves. Already in virtue of this rather simple feature—that the fact that a power's manifestation is partly physical or has has a physical effect does not imply that this power is physical one—powers can bridge the putative divide between mental and physical, thereby undercutting the very setup from which the problem of

23. See note 20.

mental causation arose.[24] Adopting a power-based account of causality thus brings with it the hope that mental causation might be no more problematic than other forms of causation. Given how ubiquitous a feature of our world mental causation appears to be, this is another attractive feature of such account.

4.6 CONCLUSIONS

Causality plays a crucial role in every attempt to explain the fabric of the world. However, as we have seen in this chapter, there is no agreement among philosophers about how to account for causation. We have examined the main alternatives in the debate, tracing them back to Aristotle and Hume. We have seen that an account of causation based on realism about powers has the resources to overcome key issues that contine to afflict Humeanism. The advantages of the former emerged also in relation to the debate on mental causation, where realism about powers would allow us to avoid the influential *causal exclusion* argument.

*

24. For other ways in which a model of causation based on the realization of powers could turn the tables on Kim's argument see Mayr (2011, ch. 9, and 2017).

▼

DETERMINISM AND

FREE WILL

5.1 INTRODUCTION

The problem of free will has continued to puzzle philosophers at least since late antiquity, though it is only in the seventeenth century that it took its distinctively modern form. It is hardly surprising that this problem has haunted philosophers for so long. It is not only a theoretical puzzle that brings out—or at least appears to bring out—major contradictions in some of our deeply rooted beliefs and intuitively plausible views about the world. It also threatens to undermine our self-understanding as moral agents and as persons.

In our ordinary thinking about ourselves and about how we lead our lives, it seems obvious to us that we are free; that it is *we* who choose—at least up to a point—how we act and live. And this fact not only seems obvious to us, it is also highly important to how we conceive of ourselves and to what we value. It greatly matters to us whether we are free in shaping our lives or not. For if we were not free in what we do, how could we be responsible for it; feel pride in our achievements or guilt about our failings; feel that we have deserved praise or blame; or even regard our lives as autonomously lived, rather than seeing ourselves just as passive puppets at the mercy of external influences?

But while it seems both obvious and highly important to us that we are free, fundamental worries easily arise concerning how we *can* be free and how it can be *us* (i.e., *we ourselves*) who determine what lives we lead. Such worries can arise from views that many philosophers have held to be part and parcel of a naturalistic world view (especially the idea that things that happen in nature must either be determined by natural laws or else be a matter of mere chance); but they can also be general worries concerning the very coherence of the idea that we can truly determine our own lives ourselves; or pertain to more specific neurological findings, which have been taken to establish that our conscious decisions are irrelevant to how our actions come about. To briefly summarize the most popular instances of each kind of puzzle:

a) *The classic free will and determinism problem:* Free will requires that we could have acted otherwise. But the course of nature, according to one highly influential view in modern science and philosophy, is determined by strict and deterministic laws. And these laws rule out all possible courses but one—namely, the one that actually occurs. So how could we really have acted otherwise, if determinism is true? (The most famous version of this worry is Peter Van Inwagen's consequence argument, which we will look at in more detail in section 5.3.)

b) *The paradox of self-creation:* Free will requires that we determine what we do and how we live—rather than being determined to do so by external or prior causal factors. But whenever I decide something, I do so on the basis of what I already am, namely on the basis of my present desires, preferences, and values. However, what I already am, must also, in its turn, be due to something. Either it is due to me—but then, it seems, I need to have decided earlier to be the way I am now, and so the very same problem comes up again at the second stage. Or, what I am is due to something else. But that seems to imply that when my decisions and actions are apparently self-determined, they are *really and ultimately* determined by these further factors—and we end up with determination "at one remove," so to speak. (This problem was pressed, in particular, by Galen Strawson 1994.)

c) *The Libet experiment:* A famous experiment by Benjamin Libet, which has been at the center of a major controversy in the last two decades, has been taken by many philosophers to show that our conscious decisions are in fact mere epiphenomena which do not (contrary to what we would usually think) initiate our actions (Libet 1985). In the experiment, participants were requested to report when they were aware of a decision that they were asked to take concerning performing a certain action (such as moving one's finger in a certain way). At the same time, their so-called "readiness potential " (a neurophysiological potential built up before, and leading to, the action) was registered. The experimental findings showed that the build-up of the readiness potential was detectable *before* the participants in the test were aware of taking any decision to perform the action in question. This showed, Libet suggested, that conscious decisions did not cause our actions, and did not enable the agent to initiate an action; but, at best, gave her the possibility to "block" an action (or to "veto" it) once she had become conscious that the action was about to occur.

In this final chapter we want to address at least some of these problems, especially those that are directly related to the philosophical issues we have discussed earlier in the book. (We will set aside specific problems about free will that arise from suggested empirical findings such as the Libet experiments.) In doing so, we will focus on one particular conception of free will of long standing in the philosophical debate, namely the understanding of free will as the capacity to choose and act otherwise. According to this conception of free will, having free will means that one is able to act and decide otherwise than one eventually does act and decide. This is not the only possible understanding of free will, though an important group of philosophers in the free-will debate are happy to consider this as the understanding suggested by "common sense and tradition" (Vihvelin 2013, 90). An important alternative understanding connects free will more directly to moral responsibility, but while we will consider this view in section 5.4, it will not be the strand in the free-will debate that we will chiefly be interested in here.

In section 5.2, we will look briefly at the history of the two main opposing positions in the free-will debate, compatibilism and incompatibilism. We will then proceed to examine the most influential argument for incompatibilism in the twentieth century (section 5.3), the so-called Consequence Argument, before we consider some compatibilist replies and counterarguments. In section 5.4, we will look at an influential argument against the connection between moral responsibility and the ability to do otherwise; if successful, this argument would either sunder the connection between free will and moral responsibility, or else suggest a different understanding of free will. In section 5.5, we will turn to the question of how the revival of interest in powers, at whose consequences for other areas of metaphysics we have already looked earlier, impinges on the incompatibilism/compatibilism stand-off.

5.2 A BRIEF HISTORY OF COMPATIBILISM AND INCOMPATIBILISM

Compatibilists and incompatibilists are divided on the question of whether free will (understood as the freedom to do otherwise) is (or would be) possible when everything that happens in nature is (or was) completely determined by prior events and natural laws. This debate had some forerunners: in particular, philosophers in the Middle Ages were concerned about whether the freedom of human agents was compatible with God's omnipotence and omniscience. But the compatibility problem in the form in which it has dominated the twentieth-century debate (i.e. as a specific problem about the compatibility of freedom with *physical* determinism, which is based on natural laws) only took philosophical center stage in early modern philosophy, when the idea of strict, deterministic laws of nature began to gain a continuously growing number of adherents. The first major philosophical debate that examined this problem in a recognizably modern form can be found in the seventeenth century, in the controversy between Thomas Hobbes and Bishop Bramhall; interestingly, their exchange already contained, at least *in nuce*, several of the considerations that were to become standard elements in the stand-off between compatibilists and incompatibilists for the next three and half centuries. Even though Hobbes did not believe that the will itself could be free, but only the person who was acting, he provided one of the first formulations of modern compatibilism when he argued that freedom should be understood in terms of the absence of external constraints. Thus understood, freedom was not restricted to human beings, but could also be ascribed to some inanimate things: for example, to the water in a river that was flowing downhill (i.e., taking its natural course) without any impediments or obstacles. With regard to human beings, however, Hobbes thought that freedom consisted in the dependence of one's actions on one's will, that is, roughly, in the ability to translate one's will into action and to do what one willed. As Hobbes puts it in *Leviathan*:

> A Free-Man, is he, that in those things, which by his strength and wit he is able to do, is not hindered to do what he has a will to. (ch. 21)

This kind of freedom, it is easy to see, is not at odds with universal determinism or "necessity" (which Hobbes considered to obtain, too): my will could be deterministically influenced by earlier factors, without this kind of determination in any way undermining my freedom on the Hobbesian account, since this freedom only concerns the relationship between will and action and completely brackets the question of how my will itself has been formed. But while this kind of freedom is compatible with determinism, it has been the continuing worry of incompatibilists that it is not robust enough and far too marginal to be of any genuine interest. It seems, as Immanuel Kant once put it with regard to a related compatibilist view, too much like the "freedom of a turnspit" (*Critique of Practical Reason*, 97), which can turn in the way it is pushed by someone, but isn't thereby free in any interesting sense. In particular, the turnspit's freedom is definitely not the kind of freedom that we think is distinctive of human beings , and that would justify the importance that freedom has for us and the related feelings of shame, desert, responsibility, and pride in our achievements.

Whether convincing or not, Hobbes's proposal was the first influential modern attempt to provide an account of freedom that was compatible with the assumption of general causal determinism. Such compatibilist attempts became more and more frequent, as the idea of strict physical laws completely determining the course of events in nature became more and more compelling with the development of physics in the late seventeenth and eighteenth centuries (with Newton's laws of motion setting an important milestone in this development). If the thought that the world is governed by general deterministic laws is a genuine and even plausible option, then freedom in the sense of the possibility of acting otherwise would either become illusory or would have to be understood in a way that did not include that the agent, *under the very same circumstances*, could have acted otherwise. It would have to be understood in a way that does not equate freedom with "freedom of indifference," as David Hume called it, where the latter would include a lack of causal determination of one's decision and action.

(*Treatise of Human Nature*, 407. Hume himself thought that the relevant freedom was only the "freedom of spontaneity," which required the absence of *external* coercion, but was not undermined by causal determination *per se*.)

One way to combine freedom with determinism in the latter way, which was made popular, at least among compatibilists, by the work of G. E. Moore (1912) at the turn to the twentieth century, was based on a conditional analysis of the relevant ability to do otherwise. Moore suggested that a statement like

(1)　I could have done otherwise.

was to be understood as shorthand for

(2)　I would have done otherwise, if I had decided (or wanted, or preferred) to do so.

This proposal of reading statements like (1) was not *ad hoc*. Moore could point to the fact that many everyday statements of the form "*A* could have done X"—that is, many statements that do not specifically concern philosophical questions about free action or free will—can plausibly be interpreted in a conditional way. "You could easily have knocked down the vase," when said after you have just violently turned around and brushed against the vase, may plausibly be taken to mean something like "If you had been nearer the vase, you would have knocked it down."

At the same time, the suggested conditional understanding of the freedom to do otherwise makes freedom compatible with determinism. For,

(2)   I would have done otherwise, if I had decided to do so.

is compatible with

(3)   It was determined by prior causal factors that I would not
      do otherwise.

since (2) is compatible with

(4)   It was determined by prior causal factors that I would not
      decide to do otherwise.

The reason is that it may be precisely due to the determination of my preferences and decisions that prior causal factors determined what I would do. So long as the relevant causal deterministic chain was running via my decisions or preferences, (2) is compatible with determinism. As a consequence, even if my preferences and decisions were themselves determined by prior causal factors, this would not exclude the relevant "conditional" freedom as expressed by (2)—not even if, as a result of this earlier determination, my action was causally determined, too.

Conditional analyses were never universally accepted, and the adequacy of (2) as an analysis of (1) was never beyond dispute. Thus, Keith Lehrer (1968) argued that (2) was even compatible with the falsity of (1) and therefore could not count as an adequate analysis of this statement. For (2) was compatible with

(5)   I could *only* have done otherwise if I had decided otherwise
      than I did.

and

(6)   I could not decide otherwise.[1]

But (5) and (6) jointly entail the negation of (1). These problems for the conditional analysis took however a significant time to change the course of the debate. One reason for this was that for a long time many philosophers didn't really see any promising (compatibilist or incompatibilist) alternative to a conditional understanding of freedom—so one could only hope that with sufficient refinements the conditional analyses might eventually be made to work. So, at least as far as the actual development of the debate was concerned, conditional analyses gave compatibilists an edge over incompatibilists in the free will debate in early analytic philosophy, and this situation persisted well into the second half of the twentieth century. The problems for incompatibilism were aggravated by a widespread suspicion that incompatibilists were either committed to mysterious extra metaphysical assumptions or else left the agent no better off in terms of self-determination than she would be in a completely deterministic scenario. For if every natural event was assumed to be either causally determined by prior causal factors or else a matter of chance, it seemed that, by claiming that free actions and decisions were not causally determined, incompatibilists were turning them into a matter of mere chance. And chance hardly seemed a better ground for self-determination than determinism: if something I did

---

1. Lehrer made this point by reference to the example of someone being unable to decide to take a red-colored candy because it reminds him of a drop of blood (1968, 32).

was due to pure chance, it was no more under *my* control and could no more be ascribed to me as *my* action than if it was determined by external factors. This problem is called the *luck objection* against incompatibilism. In order to turn freedom into something more than mere chance, incompatibilists had to provide some additional positive explanation of what freedom consisted in, to make it more than the mere absence of determination. But this, many philosophers of the mid-twentieth-century thought, would lead to positing some mysterious contra-causal influence of the agent, which was unacceptable within a "reputable" naturalistic metaphysical framework.

The compatibilist tide only turned in the 1960s and 1970s, when incompatibilists began both to offer models to answer the luck objection and new influential arguments against the compatibility of freedom and determinism appeared in the debate. While the most important model of the first kind was the so-called agent-causal model of free action, the most important new argument against compatibilism was Peter Van Inwagen's *consequence argument*, which we will turn to in the next section.

5.3 THE *CONSEQUENCE ARGUMENT* AND THE FORTUNES OF INCOMPATIBILISM

One major attraction of Van Inwagen's *consequence argument* was that it did not seem to rely on any problematic or demanding notions of determinism or freedom in order to reach its conclusion that freedom and determinism were incompatible. Rather, it seemed to use only fairly uncontroversial premises that philosophers on both sides of the compatibilist/incompatibilist divide could easily agree on. Van Inwagen took the essence of determinism to be captured by the idea that any full description of the world at one particular instance of time t, in conjunction with the laws of nature, entails the full description of the world for any later point of time t*.[2] This fairly uncontroversial formulation of determinism (which doesn't include any claim about laws of nature "governing" or "directing" the course of events) would already rule out, according to Van Inwagen, that I could ever act otherwise than I actually do (or did) act.

Imagine that you just stretched your right leg a moment ago (at time t*). If you were able to do otherwise than stretch your right leg at t*, you must have been capable of rendering the proposition "X stretched her right leg at time t* " false. But could you have rendered this proposition false if universal determinism is true? Van Inwagen thinks not. For, as he succinctly sums up his argument:

> If determinism is true, then our acts are the consequences of the laws of nature and events in the remote past. But it is not up to us what went on before we were born, and neither it is up to us what the laws of nature are. Therefore, the consequences of these things (including our present acts) are not up to us. (Van Inwagen 2003, 39)

Let us examine the steps of this argument a bit more closely. According to determinism,

---

2. As a matter of fact, Van Inwagen thought that for determinists, the entailment would run from later to earlier states, too, but this direction of entailment was irrelevant for his argument.

(7)   For any times t, t' (with t' later than t), a full description of the world at t in conjunction with the proposition expressing the laws of nature L, entails a full description of the world at t'.

Now, take a time t which was long before your birth, and the proposition "X stretched her right leg at time t*" (with t* being the time a few minutes ago). If (7) is true, then this latter proposition is among the propositions that are implied by the conjunction of a full description of the world at t and L. Since this is so, Van Inwagen thinks, you could only render false the proposition "X stretched her right leg at time t*" if you were capable of rendering false either of the two conjuncts by which the proposition is implied, by rendering false either L (i.e., the statement of the laws of nature) or the description of the world at t. But neither of these two things, Van Inwagen argues, can reasonably be supposed to be something you could ever do. Rendering false the statement of the laws of nature seems to require that you are free to break the natural laws or to work a miracle. At least for ordinary human beings it seems absurd to assume they could do either. Nor are prospects any better when we turn to your capacity for rendering false the description of the state of the world at t. For, remember, t is supposed to be a time before your birth. It seems obvious that you could not—neither when you were stretching your leg just now, or, indeed, at *any* point in your life—do anything about the state of the world *back then* or somehow retroactively influence what had happened before your birth. These past events, it seems obvious, were for you always fixed, and the propositions describing their occurrence had their truth values definitely determined long before you ever came onto the scene. So if it is true that

(8)   You can only render false the proposition "X stretched her right leg at t"' if you can render false (at least) one of the conjuncts that jointly entail it.

then it does seem that Van Inwagen is right and that determinism does exclude your ability to do otherwise. For then you could not render false the proposition in question (or, indeed, any proposition about how you have acted at some time), because it seems you could render false neither the description of the earlier state of the world nor the statement of the laws of nature.

As we have already noted, Van Inwagen's argument was so powerful and influential because both its premises and the relevant notions which were used—such as the characterization of determinism and the notion of "rendering false"—seemed fairly uncontroversial. Compatibilists however have argued that this only appears so. In particular, David Lewis has argued that the notion of "rendering false" used in Van Inwagen's argument is importantly ambiguous, and that there is a sense of this notion in which it is not absurd to suppose that we could render false the statement of the laws of nature (or, for that matter, we can add, a statement about the faraway past). According to Lewis, we should distinguish between a strong and a weak sense of "I could have rendered p false." On the strong sense, rendering p false requires performing an act such that p is made false either by the act itself or by a causal consequence of it. On the weak sense, by contrast, it only requires that I could do something such that, if I performed that act, p would have to *be* false (but not necessarily made false by the act itself or its consequences) (Lewis 2003, 127). Take the proposition "Pompeii was destroyed by an eruption of Vesuvius in 79 A.D."—could you have rendered that false at any time? In the strong sense of "rendering false," certainly not, for nothing you could ever have done, or could do now, would have prevented the Vesuvius's eruption back then or would have protected Pompeii from its consequences. However, in the weaker sense of "rendering false," there was something you could have done: for example, take a walk this morning through the intact streets of Pompeii with all the houses built in 75 A.D. still standing. For, you could not have taken this walk, unless the proposition "Pompeii was destroyed by an outbreak of the Vesuvius in 79 A.D." had been false.

Using this distinction between a strong and weak sense of "rendering false," Lewis argues that it is only clearly wrong that we can render (or could ever have rendered) false the statement of the laws of nature if we understand "rendering false" in the strong sense. If we could do so in the strong sense, then indeed we would be miracle-workers. But being able to render false the statement of the laws of nature in the weak sense does not require miraculous powers on our part. For, as Lewis argues, "all the requisite law-breaking" could be "over and done with" before I acted. All that was needed was "that my act would be preceded by another event—the divergence miracle—that would falsify a law" (Lewis, 2003, 127). (Just as you would not have needed any miraculous powers to walk through Pompeii this morning if the town had still been intact.)

Now, even though being able to render false (in the weak sense) a proposition that I do this-and-that may not, if Lewis is right, require that I have miraculous powers, you may think that this is not a major improvement as long as *some* law-breaking event (or miracle) is needed in order for you to be capable of rendering false the proposition that you stretched your right leg at t*. Law-breaking, you may think, is bad enough, *whoever* or *whatever* is responsible for it. But if you have that worry, it may help to switch to the other conjunct, which according to determinism is needed to infer the proposition about your action (i.e., your stretching your leg at t*); that is, the proposition about the past state of the world. Here it is much easier to imagine a different past state of the world, from which an action of yours which was different from the one that actually occurred would have followed. If determinism is true, you could only have acted differently just now if the remote past had been different too. But as long as you could have acted differently, this would also mean that you could have rendered false the statement about the remote past, at least in Lewis's weak sense. For then you could have done something that would have guaranteed that a past state of the world would have been different from how it actually was and therefore that the description of that past state that is actually true would have been false. (It might be true, for instance, that you could only have done something else than stretching your right leg a few minutes ago, if a volcano had broken out one year before your birth – which did not, in fact, break out. Then, if you had remained still, one could have inferred that this volcano *had* broken out back then and that the past had been different from what it actually was. In *that* sense, your action would have "changed the past"—but that is a sense which does not require any magical powers on your part.)

So it is not as absurd as it might at first appear to suppose that human agents are capable of rendering false the remote past, and by latching onto Lewis's weak sense of "rendering false," compatibilists may be able to block one essential premise in Van Inwagen's argument. But this is not the only premise that has been subject to criticism. Also, statement (8) may be much less obvious than it seems. Statement (8) gets its initial plausibility from the idea that if *x* is unavoidable or necessary for me and if *x* implies something else *y*, then *y* too must be unavoidable or necessary for me. For then I can do nothing about *x*; and clearly I cannot do anything about the implication relation either, for that solely depends on logic. But is it really true that something like the following holds?

> (9)   If it is fixed or necessary for me whether p, and necessary that if p then q, then it is also fixed or necessary for me whether q.

(Principles like (9) transfer modal status (necessity in this case) from the antecedent to the consequent of the conditional; hence they are often called "transference principles.") This will depend on the sense of "necessary" or "being fixed" at play here. If we understand it as "I cannot do anything about whether it is true or not," (9), taken as a universal principle, seems dubious. This is more easily seen if we look at cases where q is a temporal or causal *antecedent* of p rather than the other way around. Assume that p is "I am alive at 5 p.m. today" and q is "I do not commit suicide at 3 p.m. today." It is true that p entails q: if I am alive at 5 p.m., I cannot have committed suicide two hours earlier. This is something I cannot do anything about. We can also imagine that I cannot do anything about whether I am alive at 5 p.m. or not—for whether or not I commit suicide at 3 p.m., a hired killer will shoot me in any case at 4 p.m. So whatever I do,

I will not be alive at 5 p.m. But this doesn't mean that I cannot do anything about whether I commit suicide at 3 p.m. or not. That is still "up to me." So, even Van Inwagen's "transfer" principle may not be as straightforward as it seems at first. But despite its difficulties, the consequence argument did a lot to turn the predominantly compatibilist tide in the 1980s and 1990s. While compatibilists were usually not persuaded by it, at least the argument provided a major challenge which they had to face up to in order to maintain their position.

As we have already noted, there was a second major factor that further contributed to the revival of incompatibilist fortunes, namely that incompatibilists started to develop answers to the *luck objection* that were meant to show how an action or decision need not be turned into a mere matter of chance by the absence of causal determination. Two such models should be briefly mentioned here. First, incompatibilists such as Robert Kane have argued that incompatibilism does not exclude causation by prior events altogether, but only deterministic causation.[3] According to Kane, deterministic causation, where the cause makes it necessary, under the circumstances, that the effect occurs, is only one kind of causation. There is also indeterministic causation, where the cause only makes occurrence of the effect probable to some degree (with a probability-value lower than full certainty). As long as the agent's decision and action were caused only indeterministically, nothing excludes that there was a genuine possibility that the agent would have acted otherwise; that he would have acted otherwise will only have been (fairly) improbable. Indeterministic causation was

3. See Kane (1996).

also, so Kane claimed, a well-established player in theories of causation, if only because microphysical processes in quantum mechanics are (according to the majority view at least) not governed by strict deterministic laws, but rather by probability distributions. Applying this understanding of indeterministic causation to the case of free actions, Kane (and others) have argued that such causation would provide the "golden middle" path between mere chance, which would exclude the agent's control, and determinism, which would exclude alternative possibilities, and thereby give incompatibilists exactly what they wanted.

Other incompatibilists, however, were wary of this claim, since they thought that even if my decisions were caused only indeterministically in the way described, this would not put me *in control.* For as long as it wasn't *me* who could determine which of the different possible courses of events was realized, it was, from my point of view, still mere chance which course was realized.[4] In order to ensure that it was *the agent herself* who determined which course of events was realized, many of these theorists turned to the notion of agent-causation (e.g., Chisholm 1964; O'Connor 2000). According to this view, it is the agent herself, *qua* substance, that causes her own action, decision, or bodily movement. This kind of causation, it is thought, cannot be reduced to the event-causal influence of the agent's mental or physical states, or to the causal influence of events happening outside the agent's body. It is precisely this irreducibility that makes agent-causation such a promising candidate for incompatibilists to turn to, for if agent-causation turned out to be event-causation in disguise,

---

4. E.g., O'Connor (2000, chap. 2).

then the "old" worries concerning how event-causation could put the agent in control, would immediately resurface. If this event-causation was deterministic, it would exclude alternative possibilities; if indeterministic, it would not fully answer the *luck objection*.

While the jury about the viability of agent-causal accounts is still out, it should be noted that such views have received considerable support from the rise of the new realism about powers and Aristotelian models of causation we have discussed in chapters 2 and 4.[5] For if we can understand (at least many instances of) causation in terms of the exercise of the causal powers of substances, this will give us a good sense in which the substances whose causal powers are being exercised are the "sources" of the ensuing effect and will make it a plausible move to identify them as causes of this effect. This latter identification will be even more compelling if one accepts the distinction between active and passive powers which was suggested in section 4.4; and one identifies just the "active" substances as the causes: these substances are actively bringing about effects, rather than just passively undergoing changes. The substance, and in the case of agent-causation the acting person, will, however, not only be causes to whom a certain effect is due on this model. They may, in addition, be *free* causes, if the active powers in question are such that they do not *have* to be exercised under given conditions or that their exercise cannot be determined by causal antecedents. Nothing in our understanding of powers itself rules out that there can be powers of this kind; indeed, the Aristotelian tradition has emphasized the distinction between disposition-powers

5. For two models of agent-causation which both use Aristotelian powers, though in crucially different ways, see O'Connor (2009) and Mayr (2011).

and two-way powers, which we could equally well exercise or refrain from exercising under given circumstances. If the agent's active power belongs to the latter class, the power's exercises will be free, and could fail to occur under the given circumstances, which would ensure that the agent could have acted otherwise. Realism about powers thus holds the promise of a viable view of agent-causation, which explains both how what is happening is due to the agent, rather than to chance (because the agent is the cause of what happens) and, at the same time, how the agent may have been truly able to act otherwise.

5.4 MORAL RESPONSIBILITY AND FREE WILL

One of the main reasons why we are interested in free will is clearly its (presumed) connection to moral responsibility. It matters to us whether we have free will, because being free in the sense of being capable of choosing and acting otherwise seems a necessary prerequisite for being truly responsible for what we do, and for deserving praise and blame. How could we be genuinely responsible, if there were no alternatives available to us between which we could have chosen? How can one praise or blame someone for what she did if it was the only thing she *could* do and the only course of action open to her? That the answer to these questions should be "Not at all" appears highly plausible when we look at many ordinary life cases where moral criticism can be successfully warded off by saying "I couldn't help it" or "I couldn't do otherwise." When I am sitting on the beach while someone is drowning, I cannot be blamed for letting him drown if I couldn't save him because

I cannot swim or because I was e.g. somehow tied to my chair. When someone has thrown me off a roof and I fall onto a group of people on the pavement and severely injure some of them, I cannot be blamed for causing these injuries if I couldn't change the direction of my fall. The accident, we would say, was something "I couldn't help," and *therefore* it would be wrong to blame me for it. Even when the impossibility to act otherwise does not stem from external circumstances or physical incapacity, but *from myself* and my own desires and character, we allow that such incapacity can excuse the agent from blame (though in that case we are usually skeptical about whether he could truly not have acted otherwise). We do, for instance, sometimes think that a kleptomaniac is overcome by such a strong desire to steal that she cannot help stealing (even though such cases may be much rarer in reality than philosophers tend to think), and in these cases we do assume that he is not responsible for what he is doing.

Generalizing from such cases, the following *principle of alternative possibilities* (PAP) has seemed intuitively compelling to many philosophers:

> PAP: An agent is morally responsible for doing X only if she could have done otherwise than do X (i.e., refrained from doing X).

Obviously, as it stands, PAP needs some further refinement, both to cover omissions, and also to specify the availability of *which kind* of alternative options would satisfy the principle. Presumably, not *any* alternatives open to the agent will do; rather, these alternatives must be sufficiently robust, and sufficiently different from the action that the agent actually performed. For example, that the kleptomaniac could have stolen a different copy of the same book which she stole would not be enough to satisfy PAP and to ensure that she can be blamed for stealing. But leaving these issues aside here, PAP seems, at least in its essence, intuitively plausible and was almost undisputed in the free-will debate of the twentieth century until the 1960s.

But is PAP really compelling? One important line of attack against PAP has been based on certain cases of morally right actions, where an *agent cannot but do the right thing* (e.g., Wolf 1990). Think of Mother Theresa, who is so good that she cannot but help the poor people in slums who come to her to beg for her support. Given her saintly character, Mother Theresa cannot decide not to help—this is not an option open to her. But can we not still rightly morally praise and commend her for helping? Would it not be somehow unfair if she ceased to deserve this praise for doing good things just because she is *too* good?

While such cases of "moral sanctity" raise serious doubts concerning whether PAP is valid for *all* cases of moral responsibility, they do not yet undermine PAP in the area where it has its natural place as it were and its greatest intuitive appeal, namely the area of moral wrongdoing. All the specific cases we had mentioned earlier did concern cases where the agent had *prima facie* done something wrong and could ward off moral criticism by claiming that s/he could not have done otherwise. So, bracketing cases where moral praise and morally good actions are at stake, can we not uphold PAP at least for the area of moral wrongdoing, and accept that the absence of alternative possibilities at least excludes moral *blame*? Unfortunately however, not even this more modest claim is beyond dispute. This is mainly due to a famous type of counterexample that Harry Frankfurt introduced into the debate in his paper "Alternate Possibilities and Moral Responsibility" (1969).

Frankfurt's cases suggested that agents could be morally responsible for doing X even if they could not have done otherwise. The crucial feature of Frankfurt's examples is that as these cases are set up the factors that make it impossible for the agent to act otherwise than she does—i.e. the factors that exclude alternative possibilities—do not play any actual role in how the action comes about. In one popular version, which involves a neuroscientist Black and his "victim" Jones, Black very much wants Jones to shoot the President. Being a very capable neuroscientist, Black has implanted in Jones's brain a mechanism capable both of detecting in advance whether Jones will decide to shoot the President or not and of intervening in Jones's brain processes, if necessary, so as to ensure that Jones will shoot the President, even if he wouldn't decide to do it on his own. The way the case is conceived, however, Black would prefer not to show his hand and would prefer that Jones decides on his own to kill the President. For this reason, the mechanism in Jones's brain will be triggered to actually intervene and make Jones shoot the President only if the mechanism detects that Jones on his own would decide *not* to shoot the President. If it detects that Jones will decide to shoot the President on his own anyway, the mechanism will remain inactive. Now imagine that Jones does decide to shoot the President on his own. Given the presence of the mechanism in Jones's brain, it was impossible that Jones did otherwise than shoot the President. For either Jones decided, on his own, to shoot the President, or else the mechanism would have made him do it. But, despite this absence of alternative possibilities, Frankfurt argued, Jones is still morally responsible when he decides on his own. For

Black's mechanism didn't play any actual role at all in Jones's decision and action:

> Everything happened just as it would have happened without Black's presence in the situation and without his readiness to intrude into it. (Frankfurt 1969, 173)

If this is correct, then PAP is untenable even for cases of moral wrongdoing, for Jones's moral responsibility for shooting the President will not depend on its being possible for Jones to refrain from killing the President. Indeed, Frankfurt suggests, the absence of alternative possibilities cannot exclude moral responsibility *per se*. It only excludes responsibility if, in addition, the agent did what she did *only because* she could not do otherwise. This additional condition is, crucially, not fulfilled in the Black-and-Jones case, but is presumably fulfilled in the three examples which we looked at earlier when considering the initial plausibility of PAP.

Frankfurt's cases and their putative undermining of PAP profoundly changed the course of the free will debate: not only by suggesting that the highly intuitive principle PAP might well be false, but also by showing that—contrary to received opinion—in talking about free will (in the sense of an ability to do or decide otherwise) we need not be automatically talking about moral responsibility as well, or *vice versa*. As long as PAP could be assumed to be unproblematically true, free will and moral responsibility did not have to be strictly distinguished. The Frankfurt cases make it necessary to decide whether to separate the two: either (i) taking free will to be just the capacity to do otherwise, and moral responsibility to be something quite different; or (ii) distinguishing free will from the capacity to do otherwise, while keeping it intrinsically connected with moral responsibility. If one goes down the first route, the issue of compatibilism and incompatibilism arises as a separate issue for the two distinct phenomena of free will and moral responsibility. This has led philosophers such as John Martin Fischer and Mark Ravizza to develop a novel position known as "semicompatibilism", which denies that free will is compatible with universal determinism, but agrees that (roughly for the reasons pointed out by Frankfurt) moral responsibility is. Whether one should take one of these routes, depends, of course, on whether Frankfurt's cases are really successful in undermining PAP. The philosophers who have been most prominent in denying that they are, are for the most part incompatibilists. This is unsurprising, since PAP has played a key role in many arguments against the compatibility of moral responsibility and determinism. We should therefore look at some of the responses that these incompatibilists have given to Frankfurt's cases.

Several incompatibilists were quick to point out that in saying that Jones "could not have done otherwise," Frankfurt moves too swiftly. True: Jones could not have avoided killing the President, for Black would have made sure that he would kill the President anyway. But there is something Jones could still have avoided, namely *killing the President on his own, or the President's being killed as a result of a free decision of Jones's* (see, e.g., O'Connor 2000, 19). For if Jones had not been about to decide on his own to kill the President, Black's mechanism would have intervened; by intervening, it would have ruled out a free decision on Jones's part, and in the alternative scenario that would then have ensued, Jones would not have killed the President on his own, but as a "puppet" in Black's hands. So there is something that Jones could have avoided even in Frankfurt's example—and is that not enough to say that Jones could have acted otherwise and that PAP is satisfied? Opinions on this point remain divided. Compatibilists such as John Martin Fischer and Mark Ravizza have replied that alternatives like "killing the President as a puppet in Black's hands" provide mere "flickers of freedom" that are not sufficiently robust to ground responsibility (1998, 100). In particular, it is argued, the alternatives that are open to Jones are insufficiently robust, because they are all alternatives in which Jones acts *unfreely*. It is very difficult to decide when an alternative is robust enough for its availability to ground moral responsibility. But perhaps understanding *what exactly* Jones is meant to be responsible for in Frankfurt's case helps us at least to finesse this question. Look again at

> PAP: An agent is morally responsible for doing X only if she could have done otherwise than do X (i.e., refrained from doing X).

We use one and the same variable ("X"), for which we can substitute action descriptions, in both the antecedent and the consequent of the conditional. If Jones was responsible for performing an action of a particular kind Y, even if he could not avoid performing an action of this very kind Y, then PAP is false. If, by contrast, he is, strictly speaking, responsible for something else than what he could not avoid doing—that is, if in Frankfurt's cases we, strictly speaking, have to substitute two different action-descriptions in the antecedent and the consequence of PAP—then PAP can be maintained and the original example will turn out to be just misleading. So what exactly is Jones responsible for in Frankfurt's case? Frankfurt thinks it is "shooting the President," and if this is correct, then PAP is refuted because "shooting the President" is also what

Jones cannot avoid doing. Alternatively, Jones might not be responsible for "shooting the president"—given that he couldn't help *that*—but might only be responsible for something else, for example, for deciding to shoot the President because he hates him. The latter is something that Jones *could* have avoided, because had Black's mechanism forced Jones to shoot the President, Jones's own hatred wouldn't have played any role in his decision. So whether Frankfurt's case against PAP is successful hinges on whether Frankfurt is right in thinking that what Jones is genuinely responsible for is "shooting the President" or not. Ordinary parlance seems to bear out Frankfurt here; but of course incompatibilists will question its reliability at this point, and we will be content with leaving this point in the balance here.

Another line of criticism against Frankfurt's examples by the incompatibilists concerns their alleged value in providing an argument against the incompatibility of moral responsibility and universal determinism. As, for example, David Widerker (2003) has argued, the example, as it stands, leaves it open whether Jones, in deciding on his own to shoot the President, would have been able to act otherwise or not. For Black's mechanism would have to pick up on some prior signal in Jones's brain in order to detect which decision Jones would take on his own. This prior signal could either be itself a deterministic cause (or the byproduct of such a cause) of Jones's later decision, or an indeterministic one. In the latter case, Jones could still have decided otherwise (even if, perhaps, the probability of his doing so was very low), despite Black's mechanism being in place. There was therefore, in this latter scenario, an alternative possibility, because the mechanism lacked a completely reliable indication of how Jones would decide. In the former case, by contrast, this possibility is excluded. But of course in this case Jones's decision was deterministically caused and is therefore a decision for which an incompatibilist doesn't consider Jones to be responsible anyway. So Frankfurt's case cannot establish that moral responsibility does not require alternative possibilities without begging the question against the incompatibilist, it seems. Either it will turn out that Jones could have done otherwise, after all, or that he wasn't morally responsible. And in neither case do we have a counterexample to PAP.

This incompatibilist response isn't however entirely successful. Later defenders of Frankfurt tried to provide modified versions of Frankfurt's case that avoid the rather technical problem of needing a signal to indicate how Jones will decide. We should also recall the general dialectic of Frankfurt's debate against the incompatibilist. Frankfurt can reply that, when the truth of PAP is at stake, the incompatibilist cannot, without herself begging the question, use this principle in order to argue for the incompatibility of moral responsibility and universal determinism. And there seems no other ground for taking determinism to rule out responsibility unless one already assumes PAP.[6] Therefore, with respect to assessing Frankfurt's argument, the incompatibilist cannot presuppose that if the decision is deterministically caused, it is one for which Jones is not morally responsible.

However, there may be another, still easier way for the incompatibilist to respond to Frankfurt's cases. The incompatibilist might just accept Frankfurt's proposal

---

6. Unless one assumes that the agent cannot be a true "source" of what she is doing when she is determined to act by prior causal factors. But we cannot go into the details of this so-called "sourcehood" (as opposed to "leeway") incompatibilism here.

concerning the restricted role of alternative possibilities, namely that the absence of alternative possibilities only rules out moral responsibility in those cases in which the agent acts as he does *only because* he cannot act otherwise. Can the incompatibilist not then argue that this additional condition is always fulfilled if universal determinism is true, because in this case the agent acts as he does precisely because earlier events and the laws of nature make it impossible for him to act otherwise (*pace* Frankfurt 1969, 175f.)?

So, even if Frankfurt's example of Black and Jones is a valid counterexample to PAP—because what Jones was morally responsible for might well be something he couldn't avoid doing—this needn't really undermine the traditional case for incompatibilism concerning moral responsibility (which might just need some modification). What Frankfurt's cases really teach us is, ultimately, not which of the compatibilist and incompatibilist sides of the debate is right; but rather that we cannot simply assume that free will, the ability to do otherwise, and moral responsibility are somehow one and the same thing. In doing so, these cases have certainly radically changed the setup of the free will debate. In the following section, we will look at another potential game-changer for this debate, namely powers.

5.5 FREE WILL AND THE "NEW DISPOSITIONALISM"

As we have already seen, the new realism about powers and dispositions has had a notable impact on the free will debate in the last twenty years. For instance, this realism can be used to flesh out certain theories of substance-causation that are used in some incompatibilist theories (i.e., agent-causal theories, section 5.3). But it can also be used by compatibilists, and how it has been used in this respect will be our topic in this section. Power metaphysics appeals to compatibilists because it enables them to explain the "could" in statements like "He could have done otherwise" in a sense that is both well-established and nonmysterious, and at the same time clearly compatible with universal determinism. This is the sense of power- or ability-ascription. One way to understand

(9)   James could have played the piano yesterday evening.

is as the ascription of a general ability to play the piano to James. James is, for example, a trained piano player, and this is enough to make (10) true. Importantly, understood in the sense of ability-ascription, (10) can be true even if external circumstances yesterday evening were such that James could not exercise his general ability to play the piano (e.g., because he was somewhere where there was no piano at hand). Since, uncontroversially, general abilities can be possessed in a fully deterministic world, (10) in this sense is compatible with determinism, even when James did not actually play the piano yesterday evening. Thus compatibilists may point out that even in a deterministic world there is a perfectly good sense in which we *can* do otherwise, because even there we can have the general abilities that are required for acting otherwise.

It is rather implausible, though, that when we talk about the ability to do otherwise which is at stake in the free will debate and the discussion about the preconditions for moral responsibility, we are merely talking about the possession of general abilities. After all, it seems obvious that James cannot deserve moral blame for not playing the piano (even if doing so would have cheered up his friend Jane and he had a moral duty to try to cheer her up), if the only reason he did not play was that there was no opportunity for playing, for example because there was no piano around. So, the relevant "could" must be tied more closely to the particular occasion. Antony Kenny has suggested that we should understand it as the "could" of "particular" possibility, which combines both possession of a power and circumstantial possibility (1978, 30). On this view, the agent must not only have possessed the relevant general ability, but external and physical circumstances must have been such that he could have exercised it.

However, even this move might not go far enough to provide the sense of "could have done otherwise" required for free will and responsibility. On Kenny's proposal, "James could have done otherwise" is compatible with universal determinism, since James could have played the piano, in this sense, if he had the general ability to play and there was an opportunity for exercising it (there was a piano around, he didn't have a cramp in his fingers, etc.). All these features could have obtained, and James might still not have played, even when determinism is true—for example if James just didn't *want* to play and his not wanting to play determined that he wouldn't play. The "could have done otherwise" condition, on Kenny's account, is only compatible with determinism, though, because this condition, in Kenny's interpretation, abstracts from some features of the particular situation, specifically, from what the agent wants. Incompatibilists, however, will insist that in not taking into account all features of the situation (bracketing, in particular, James's desires), Kenny's account of "could" leaves out something crucial and does not capture the idea that *under the very same circumstances* James could have played the piano even if, in fact, he did not.

This insistence on the incompatibilist part reflects what is at the heart of the debate between compatibilists and incompatibilists: while the latter want an "all-in" possibility of the agent's acting otherwise—that is, that the agent could have acted otherwise, the circumstances being exactly what they were—this is something that compatibilists *cannot* provide and consider as unnecessary. (Why can compatibilists not provide this kind of alternative possibility? If determinism is true, the complete set of circumstances of the agent's actions *will* necessarily determine that he acted in one specific way.) Who is right in the debate is not something we can decide here. But what we want to stress is that the compatibilist's job, in availing herself of the resources provided by the new realism of powers, is not completed if she merely points out that power-ascriptions (or power-plus-opportunity-ascriptions) give us a well established and nonmysterious sense of "could" in which the "could have done otherwise" statements can be read. What the compatibilist also has to do is show that this sense of "could" is precisely the one that is at issue in the debate about free will and moral responsibility. (Appeal to powers thus changes the controversy into one between different senses of "could.")[7]

Furthermore, the move to "particular possibilities" in Kenny's sense may be insufficient for other reasons. For in focusing only on James's possession of the ability and the opportunity to play the piano, it brackets several features that could prevent James from playing the piano and do so by

---

7. See Whittle (2010).

undermining James's freedom and moral responsibility; in particular, defects or weaknesses of James's will. James might be unable to play because he suffers from a terrible agoraphobia, and the only available piano stands in a public square. Or James might be a helpless addict who just now has to take his dose of drugs and therefore is incapable of doing anything else. If freedom is incompatible with such defects of the will, a viable account of freedom will have to exclude cases such as these. One way to do that, which fits particularly well within a powers framework, is to posit possession of an additional meta-ability to recognize and rightly respond to reasons, as an additional necessary condition for freedom (e.g., "reasons-responsiveness" in the sense of Fischer and Ravizza 1998). Such an ability would include, as a first approximation, that the agent is capable of registering morally relevant features of a situation; capable of seeing that they speak in favor of or against certain courses of action; and capable of forming her decisions about how to act on the basis of these assessments. By including the possession of such a capacity among the conditions for freedom and responsibility, cases like the ones of the agoraphobic and the addict could be dealt with, because these cases are characterized by the fact that on account of their addictions or phobia such agents either lack an adequate understanding of their situation and of how it would be good to act, or are incapable of acting on this understanding. Nor would positing such an additional meta-ability, at least in the form of a general capacity, be *ad hoc*; it is largely uncontroversial that possession of such a capacity is required for responsibility. For instance, such possession is generally presupposed in systems of the criminal law, when it comes to criminal responsibility. People who are either generally incapable of realizing that their action is wrong, or generally incapable of forming their decisions on this basis—young children for instance—are excluded from its scope. This, of course, still leaves open several further issues, such as what precise kind of ability this meta-ability would be, but we have to set these issues aside here.

Appealing to powers has not only served to introduce a new sense of "could" into the free-will debate; as a byproduct, it has also led to new kind of response to Frankfurt's cases against PAP, that has, somewhat ironically, led to a situation in which compatibilists came to defend PAP, though this principle had normally been used in key arguments for *in*compatibilism (e.g., Smith 2004; Fara 2008). In discussing powers in chapter 2, we saw that most realists about powers accept that powers can be finked. Cases of finks, such as those proposed by C. B. Martin, were cases in which the stimulus of a disposition would also lead to loss of the disposition, but where the disposition is retained by the object as long as the stimulus doesn't occur. One example was Martin's electro-fink case, where the presence of the fink doesn't by itself make the wire go dead, even though the wire would go dead if a conductor was about to touch it. Now, as some philosophers have noted, finks can be seen as good models for thinking about Frankfurt's cases. Let us ask ourselves whether Jones, in Frankfurt's original case, has the power to do otherwise, which, in Jones's case, would be the power to decide not to kill the President. Let us assume that the relevant stimulus for this power's exercise is Jones's coming to prefer not to kill the President. So his power to decide otherwise is the power to decide not to kill the President if he prefers not to kill him. Now this power, it seems, is not lost but merely finked by the presence of Black's mechanism. Just as in Martin's case, this mechanism would be activated by the stimulus for Jones's power to decide not to kill the President. For if the mechanism were to register that Jones prefers not to kill the President, it would prevent him from forming a decision not to shoot the President, and thereby remove his power to form this decision. But as long as this mechanism is not activated, because Jones does not come to have a preference of the relevant kind, Jones's power to decide not to kill the President remains in place. So if we understand the relevant "could" in PAP as the "could" of power possession, Frankfurt's cases need not be seen as counterexamples to PAP, since they can also be interpreted as cases in which Jones's power to do otherwise is merely finked, but not yet removed, by the presence of Black's mechanism (see Fara 2008).

There is a further important impact of power realism on the debate around PAP that we would like to note here. Appeal to powers strongly supports the restriction of PAP to cases of moral wrongdoing, which we have discussed in section 5.4. As we have seen there, cases of "moral sanctity" suggest that, while alternative possibilities may be required for moral responsibility in cases of moral wrongdoing, the agent's inability to do wrong should not always exclude her responsibility when she does the morally *right* thing. But so far this was just a matter of our intuitive assessment of such cases. Thinking about PAP in terms of abilities or powers of the agent enables us to provide a systematic explanation of this asymmetry. For the possession of an ability to do X is crucially asymmetrical with regard to the possibility of doing X and the possibility of not doing X. If I have the ability to do X, then there must be at least some sense of "possible" in which it follows that it is also possible that I do X. This is just implied by my possession of this ability. But having the ability to do X does *not* equally imply that it is also possible that I fail to do X. If I am extremely good at doing X, or my ability to do X is so strong that I am practically infallible (think of my ability to add 2+2 correctly: how *could* I make a mistake there, as long as I have this ability?!), it may be the case that I have the ability to do X, but it is impossible that (at least when the conditions are right) I fail to do X.

As we have seen, the abilities that an agent will need in order to be responsible will not just be abilities to perform particular kinds of actions, but will plausibly include some kind of meta-ability to rightly respond to reasons. Rightly responding to reasons, as far as moral reasons are concerned, means acting morally rightly. Thus, if I acted morally wrongly and had the capacity to respond rightly to reasons, which is a precondition for moral responsibility, it is guaranteed that I could have acted otherwise than I did—namely, morally rightly. For, I had the ability to respond rightly to moral reasons, and reacting rightly would have been a different reaction from the one I actually exhibited; so when we read the "could" as the "could" of ability-ascription it is guaranteed that I could have done something else. By contrast, if I already acted rightly, then I did what my ability to rightly respond to reasons was an ability *for*. Therefore, at least from my possession of this ability, it does not follow that I could have acted otherwise if I was morally responsible. So we end up with an interesting asymmetry that bears out the intuitive difference between the cases of moral wrongdoing and of moral saints we had noted earlier.[8]

By giving incompatibilists about moral responsibility a new answer to the Frankfurt cases by which to defend PAP,

8. See also Wolf (1990) and Nelkin (2011).

while at the same time suggesting a restriction of this principle and a compatibilist reading of the "could" of the "could have done otherwise" condition, the metaphysics of powers has generated a major shift in the usual battle lines in the free-will debate. But as we have seen, there remain some crucial open issues concerning the nature of the powers and dispositions involved as well as the question of why the "could" of ability (and opportunity) possession should be the relevant one for understanding free will and the conditions of moral responsibility. These issues are far from conclusively settled in the current debate.

5.6 CONCLUSIONS

The problem of free will is one of the most well-known and most intensely discussed in metaphysics. As we have seen in this chapter, it is not only important in itself, but also a point of convergence for many other problems, for instance those concerning causality and modality. In this chapter we have examined the two sides of the debate between compatibilists and incompatibilists, and we have seen how recent developments in other areas of metaphysics might help to overcome some central but problematic assumptions of the traditional debate on free will and to better understand the relationship between free will and moral responsibility.

*

CONCLUSION

A never-ending task

WE DELIBERATELY WANT TO LEAVE this book's conclusion open-ended. This is because we believe that progress in philosophy consists in advancing our understanding of certain fundamental questions, such as the ones we introduced in the preceding chapters, rather than by finding any definitive answers to those questions. We advance our understanding by exploring the questions at issue, developing hypotheses to address them, offering arguments in support of our hypotheses, and finally examining their validity by "testing" them against possible counterexamples. We have tried to illustrate this method in connection with the topics investigated here: substance, properties, causation, modality, and free will. We have shown how certain questions in metaphysics have been driving philosophical inquiry since its very beginning, from antiquity through the centuries and indeed millennia that separate us from Plato and Aristotle. In looking at different attempts to answer such questions, we have noted how and why certain lines of thought appear more promising than others when arguments in support and against are weighted. One *trait d'union* of this book has been our effort to show that the metaphysics of powers and its recent revival provides us an angle from which we can fruitfully re-examine within a unified framework "traditional" questions in a variety of areas in metaphysics. We hope that even the reader who might skeptical about the neo-Aristotelian power ontology we have presented, will be able to appreciate that it is an approach that opens up novel lines of inquiry. Philosophers make progress even when they cannot reach ultimate conclusions; and when firm conclusions seem to have been established, it is the philosopher's job to be always prepared to scrutinize them afresh. Critiquing existing views and developing better ones just is participating in the ongoing project of metaphysics. And this is what we want, above all, to encourage our readers to do – and we hope that they will find it as rewarding as we do.

BIBLIOGRAPHY

Anscombe, G. E. M. (1993) "Causality and Determination", in M. Sosa and M. Tooley (eds.), *Causation*, Oxford: Oxford University Press, pp. 88–104.

Aristotle (1984) *Complete Works of Aristotle, Volumes 1 and 2*, ed. J. Barnes, The Revised Oxford Translation, Princeton: Bollingen Series.

Armstrong, D. (1997) *A World of States of Affairs*, Cambridge: Cambridge University Press.

Austin, J. L. (1979) *Philosophical Papers*, Urmson James Opie and Geoffrey James Warnock (eds.), 3rd ed. New York: Oxford University Press.

Baker, L. R. (1993) "Metaphysics and Mental Causation", in J. Heil and A. Mele (eds.), *Mental Causation*, Oxford: Oxford University Press, pp. 75–96.

Bird, A. (2007) *Nature's Metaphysics: Laws and Properties*, Oxford: Oxford University Press.

Black, M. (1952) "The Identity of Indiscernibles", *Mind*, 61, pp. 153–64.

Bradley, F. H. (1893) *Appearance and Reality*, London: George Allen & Unwin LTD.

Campbell, K. (1990) *Abstract Particulars*, Oxford: Blackwell.

Carnap, R. (1934) *The Unity of Science*, London: Kegan Paul.

Charles, D. (1984) *Aristotle's Philosophy of Action*, London: Duckworth.

Chisholm, R. M. (2003) [1964] "Human Freedom and the Self, 'The University of Kansas Lindley Lecture'", in G. Watson (ed.), *Free Will*, Oxford: Oxford University Press, pp. 26–37.

Chisholm, R. M. (1976) *Person and Object: A Metaphysical Study*, La Salle, IL: Open Court.

Clarke, R. (1996) "Agent Causation and Event Causation in the Production of Free Action", *Philosophical Topics*, 24, pp. 19–48.

Descartes, René (1982) *Principia Philosophiae, Oeuvres de Descartes VIII-1*, ed. C. Adam and P. Tannery, Paris: Librairie Philosophique J. Vrin.

Esfeld, M. (2004) "Quantum Entanglement and a Metaphysics of Relations", *Studies in History and Philosophy of Modern Physics*, 35b, pp. 601–17.

Fara, M. (2008) "Masked Abilities and Compatibilism", *Mind*, 117, pp. 843–65.

Fine, K. (1994) "Essence and Modality", *Philosophical Perspectives*, 8, pp. 1–16.

Fine, K. (2000) "Neutral Relations", *Philosophical Review*, 109, pp. 1–33.

Fine, K. (2008) "In Defence of Three-Dimensionalism", *Philosophy*, 83, suppl. 62, pp. 1–16.

Fischer, J. M., and M. Ravizza. (1998) *Responsibility and Control: A Theory of Moral Responsibility*, Cambridge: Cambridge University Press.

Frankfurt, H. (2003) [1969] "Alternate Possibilities and Moral Responsibility", in G. Watson (ed.), *Free Will*, Oxford: Oxford University Press, pp. 167–76.

Frede, M. (1987) *Essays in Ancient Philosophy*, Minneapolis: University of Minnesota Press.

Goodman, N. (1983) *Facts, Fiction and Predictions*, 4th ed., Cambridge, MA: Harvard University Press.

Harré, R., and E. Madden (1975) *Causal Powers: Theory of Natural Necessity*, Oxford: Blackwell.

Heil, J. (2003) *From an Ontological Point of View*, Oxford: Clarendon Press.

Heil, J. (2012) *The Universe as We Find It*, Oxford: Clarendon Press.

Heil, J. (2017) "Real modalities", in J. Jacobs (ed.), *Causal Powers*, Oxford: Oxford University Press, pp. 90–104.

Hobbes, T. (1991) *Leviathan*, Cambridge: Cambridge University Press.

Hume, D. (2000) *An Enquiry Concerning Human Understanding*, Oxford: Oxford University Press.

Hume, D. (2007) *A Treatise of Human Nature*, vol. I, Oxford: Oxford University Press.

Humphreys, P. (1997) "How Properties Emerge", *Philosophy of Science*, 64, pp. 1–17.

Jacobs, J. (2010) "A Powers Theory of Modality: or, How I Learned to Stop Worrying and Reject Possible Worlds", *Philosophical Studies*, 151(2), pp. 227–48.

Jaworski, W. (2016) *Structure and the Metaphysics of Mind: How Hylomorphism Solves the Mind-Body Problem*, Oxford: Oxford University Press.

Kane, R. (1996) *The Significance of Free Will*, Oxford: Oxford University Press.

Kant, I. (1900a) *Kritik der reinen Vernunft*, in Königlich-Preussische Akademie der Wissenschaften (ed.), *Kant's Gesammelte Schriften*. 29 vols. Berlin 1900–, vols. 3–4.

Kant, I. (1900b) *Kritik der praktischen Vernunft*, in Königlich-Preussische Akademie der Wissenschaften (ed.), *Kant's Gesammelte Schriften*. 29 vols. Berlin 1900–, vol. 5.

Kenny, A. (1978) *Free Will and Responsibility*, London: Routledge Kegan Paul.

Kim, J. (1993) "Causes and Counterfactuals", in E. Sosa and M. Tooley (eds.), *Causation*, Oxford: Oxford University Press, pp. 205–7.

Kim, J. (1998) *Mind in a Physical World*, Cambridge: Cambridge University Press.

Kment, B. (2017) "Varieties of Modality", *The Stanford Encyclopedia of Philosophy* (Spring 2017 edition), Edward N. Zalta (ed.), https://plato.stanford.edu/archives/spr2017/entries/modality-varieties/.

Koslicki, K. (2008) *The Structure of Objects*, Oxford: Oxford University Press.

Kripke, S. (1980) *Naming and Necessity*, Cambridge, MA: Harvard University Press.

Kripke, S. (1999) "Identity and Necessity", in J. Kim and E. Sosa (eds.), *Metaphysics: An Anthology*, Oxford: Blackwell, pp. 72–89.

Ladyman, J., and Ross, D. (2007) *Everything Must Go: Metaphysics Naturalized*, Oxford: Oxford University Press.

Lehrer, K. (1968) "Cans without Ifs", *Analysis*, 29, pp. 29–32.

Lewis, D. (1973) *Counterfactuals*, Cambridge, MA: Harvard University Press.

Lewis, D. (1986a) *On the Plurality of Worlds*, Oxford: Basil Blackwell.

Lewis, D. (1986b) *Philosophical Papers*, vol. II, Oxford: Oxford University Press.

Lewis, D. (1997) "Finkish Dispositions", *Philosophical Quarterly*, 47, pp. 143–58.

Lewis, D. (2003) "Are we Free to Break the Laws?", in G. Watson (ed.), *Free Will*, Oxford: Oxford University Press, Oxford, pp. 122–9.

Lewis, D. (2004) "Causation as Influence (unabridged version)", in J. Collins, N. Hall, and L. A. Paul (eds.), *Causation and Counterfactuals*, Cambridge, MA: MIT Press, pp. 75–106.

Libet, B. (1985) "Unconscious Cerebral Initiative and the Role of the Conscious Will in Voluntary Action", *Behavioral Brain Sciences*, 8, pp. 529–39.

Locke, J. (1975) *An Essay Concerning Human Understanding*, Oxford: Oxford University Press.

Lowe, E. J. (1998) *The Possibility of Metaphysics*, Oxford: Oxford University Press.

Lowe, E. J. (2002) *Survey of Metaphysics*, Oxford: Oxford University Press.

Lowe, E. J. (2012) "A Neo-Aristotelian Substance Ontology: Neither Relational Nor Constituent", in T. E. Tahko (ed.), *Contemporary Aristotelian Metaphysics*, Cambridge: Cambridge University Press, 229–4.

Mackie, J. L. (1974) *The Cement of the Universe: A Study of Causation*, Oxford: Clarendon Press.

Mackie, J. L. (1993) "Causation and Conditions", in E. Sosa and M. Tooley (eds.), *Causation*, Oxford: Oxford University Press, pp. 33–55.

Mackie, P. (2006) *How Things Might Have Been: Individuals, Kinds, and Essential Properties*, Oxford: Clarendon Press.

Marmodoro, A. (2007) "The Union of Cause and Effect in Aristotle Physics III", *Oxford Studies in Ancient Philosophy*, 32, pp. 205–32.

Marmodoro, A. (2013) "Aristotle's Hylomorphism without Reconditioning", *Philosophical Inquiry*, 37, pp. 5–22.

Marmodoro, A. (2014) *Aristotle on Perceiving Object*, Oxford: Oxford University Press.

Marmodoro, A. (2017a) "Aristotelian Powers at Work: Reciprocity without Symmetry in Causation", in J. Jacobs (ed.), *Causal Powers*, Oxford: Oxford University Press, pp. 57–76.

Marmodoro, A. (2017b) "Power Mereology: Structural versus Substantial Powers", In M. P. Paoletti and F. Orilia (eds.), *Philosophical and Scientific Perspectives on Downward Causation*, London: Routledge, pp. 110–27.

Marmodoro, A., and D. Yates (eds.) (2016) *The Metaphysics of Relations*, Oxford: Oxford University Press.

Marmodoro, A., and E. Mayr (2017) *Breve introduzione alla metafisica*, Rome: Carocci.

Martin, C. B. (1993) "Power for Realists", in K. Cambell, J. Bacon, and L. Reinhardt (eds.), *Ontology, Causality, and Mind: Essays on the Philosophy of D. M. Armstrong*, Cambridge: Cambridge University Press, pp. 175–86.

Martin, C. B. (1994) "Dispositions and Conditionals", *Philosophical Quarterly*, 44, pp. 1–8.

Martin, C. B., and J. Heil (1999) "The Ontological Turn", *Midwest Studies in Philosophy*, 23(1), pp. 34–60.

Mayr, E. (2011) *Understanding Human Agency*, Oxford: Oxford University Press.

Mayr, E. (2017) "Powers and Downward Causation", in M. Paolini Paoletti and F. Orilia (eds.), *Philosophical and Scientific Perspectives on Downward Causation*, London: Routledge, pp. 76–91.

Menzel, C. (2016) "Possible Worlds", in E. N. Zalta (ed.), *The Stanford Encyclopedia of Philosophy*, http://plato.stanford.edu/archives/fall2016/entries/possible-worlds/.

Menzies, C. (2014) "Counterfactual Theories of Causation", in E. N. Zalta (ed.), *The Stanford Encyclopedia of Philosophy*, http://plato.stanford.edu/archives/spr2014/entries/causation-counterfactual/.

Molnar, G. (2003) *Powers: A Study in Metaphysics*, Oxford: Oxford University Press.

Moore, A. (2012) *The Evolution of Modern Metaphysics: Making Sense of Things*, Cambridge: Cambridge University Press.

Moore, G. E. (1912) *Ethics*, Oxford: Oxford University Press.

Mumford, S., and R. L. Anjum (2011) *Getting Causes from Powers*, Oxford: Oxford University Press.

Nelkin, D. K. (2011) *Making Sense of Freedom and Responsibility*, Oxford: Oxford University Press.

O'Connor, T. (2000) *Persons and Causes: The Metaphysics of Free Will*, Oxford: Oxford University Press.

O'Connor, T. (2009) "Agent-Causal Power", in T. Handfield (ed.), *Dispositions and Causes*, Oxford: Clarendon Press, pp. 189–214.

Plantinga, A. (1979) "Actualism and Possible Worlds", in M. Loux (ed.), *The Possible and the Actual: Readings in the Metaphysics of Modality*, Ithaca, NY: Cornell University Press, pp. 253–73.

Plantinga, A. (1999) "Modalities: Basic Concepts and Distinctions", in J. Kim and E. Sosa (eds.), *Metaphysics: An Anthology*, Oxford: Blackwell, pp. 135–48.

Pollock, J. L. (1976) *Subjunctive Reasoning*, Dordrecht: Reidel.

Putnam, H. (1975) "Mind, Language and Reality", *Philosophical Papers*, Vol. 2, Cambridge: Cambridge University Press.

Quine, W. V. O. (1953a) "On What there Is", in *From a Logical Point of View*, Cambridge, MA: Harvard University Press, pp. 1–19.

Quine, W. V. O. (1953b) "Identity, Ostension and Hypostasis", in *From a Logical Point of View*, Cambridge, MA: Harvard University Press, pp. 65–79.

Quine, W. V. O. (1953c) "Reference and Modality", in *From a Logical Point of View*, Cambridge, MA: Harvard University Press, pp. 139–60.

Quine, W. V. O. (1960) *Word and Object*, Cambridge, MA: MIT Press.

Quine, W. V. O. (1981) *Theories and Things*, Cambridge, MA: Harvard University Press.

Rapp, C. (2016) *Metaphysik*, München: C. H. Beck.

Rea, M. (2011) "Hylomorphism Reconditioned", *Philosophical Perspectives*, 25, pp. 341–58.

Russell, B. (1903) *The Principles of Mathematics*, Cambridge: Cambridge University Press.

Russell, B. (1912) *The Problems of Philosophy*, Oxford: Oxford University Press.

Ryle, G. (1949) "Meaning and Necessity", *Philosophy*, 24, pp. 69–76.

Ryle, G. (1990) *The Concept of Mind*, London: Penguin.

Scaltsas, T. (1994) *Substances and Universals in Arsitotle's Metaphysics*, Ithaca, NY: Cornell University Press.

Schaffer, J. (2009) "On what grounds what", in D. Manley, D. Chalmers, and R. Wasserman (eds.), *Metametaphysics: New Essays on the Foundations of Ontology*, Oxford: Oxford University Press, pp. 347–83.

Schaffer, J. (2013) "The Action of the Whole", *Proceedings of the Aristotelian Society* Suppl. Vol. 87, pp. 67–87.

Sider, T. (2001) *Four-Dimensionalism: An Ontology of Persistence and Time*, Oxford: Oxford University Press.

Smith, M. (2004) "A Theory of Freedom and Responsibility", in *Ethics and the A Priori: Selected Essays on Moral Psychology and Meta-Ethics*, Cambridge: Cambridge University Press, pp. 84–113.

Sorabji, R. (1980) *Necessity, Cause and Blame: Perspectives on Aristotle's Theory*, London: Duckworth.

Strawson, G. (1994) "The Impossibility of Moral Responsibility", in G. Watson (ed.), *Free Will*, Oxford: Oxford University Press, pp. 212–28.

Strawson, P. F. (1959) *Individuals*, London: Methuen.

Tahko, T. E. (2012) *Contemporary Aristotelian Metaphysics*, Cambridge: Cambridge University Press.

Van Inwagen, P. (2003) "An Argument for Incompatibilism", in G. Watson (ed.), *Free Will*, Oxford: Oxford University Press, pp. 38–57.

Vetter, B. (2015) *Potentiality: From Dispositions to Modality*, Oxford: Oxford University Press.

Vihvelin, K. (2013) *Causes, Laws, and Free Will: Why Determinism Doesn't Matter*, New York: Oxford University Press.

Waterlow, S. (1982) *Nature, Change, and Agency in Aristotle's Physics*, Oxford: Oxford University Press.

Whittle, A. (2010) "Dispositional Abilities", *Philosophers' Imprint*, 10, pp. 1–23.

Widerker, D. (2003) "Libertarianism and Frankfurt's Attack on the Principle of Alternative Possibilities", in G. Watson (ed.), *Free Will*, Oxford: Oxford University Press, pp. 177–89.

Wiggins, D. (2001) *Sameness and Substance Renewed*, Cambridge: Cambridge University Press.

Witt, C. (1994) *Substance and Essence in Aristotle*, Ithaca, NY: Cornell University Press.

Wolf, S. (1990) *Freedom within Reason*, Oxford: Oxford University Press.

Yablo, S. (1992) "Mental Causation", *Philosophical Review*, 101, pp. 245–80.

INDEX